Supporting Behaviour by
Building Resilience and
Emotional Intelligence

A Guide for Classroom Teachers

SECOND EDITION

**CRITICAL
TEACHING**

CRITICAL
PUBLISHING

Supporting Behaviour by
Building Resilience and
Emotional Intelligence

A Guide for Classroom Teachers

SECOND EDITION

VICTOR ALLEN

CRITICAL
TEACHING

First edition published in 2014 by Critical Publishing Ltd

Second edition published in 2018

British Library Cataloguing in Publication Data
A CIP record for this book is available from the British Library

ISBN: 978-1-912508-00-6

This book is also available in the following e-book formats:

MOBI ISBN: 978-1-912508-01-3
EPUB ISBN: 978-1-912508-02-0
Adobe e-book ISBN: 978-1-912508-03-7

Text design by Greensplash Limited
Cover design by Out of House Limited
Project Management by Out of House Publishing
Printed and bound in Great Britain by Bell & Bain, Glasgow

Critical Publishing
3 Connaught Road
St Albans
AL3 5RX
www.criticalpublishing.com

Contents

Dedication

I dedicate this book to my wife and best friend, Sonia. Her love, help, support and encouragement helps me in all I do. She is my biggest fan and the gentlest of critics. Her friendship and companionship are my greatest pleasures and I wish to thank her for her patience as I spend time learning, writing and talking to others. Her assistance as my sounding board when I have an idea is greatly appreciated and her knowledge regarding SEND is invaluable. To all the teachers who have chosen to take up this great profession. To my two daughters Laura and Esther who helped me learn about being a dad and are such a blessing to me. I would also like to thank Helen Fairlie, whose tireless work has enabled my ideas, thoughts and words to be so clearly understood, and to Lyra and Leo, our two grandchildren, who have reminded me of all the fun of growing up.

Endorsement

I have worked with Victor for a good few years now since having the pleasure of meeting him at a conference on leadership that he was speaking at.

The reason I have continued to work with him is for his wealth of experience and expertise in getting right to the root of issues – whether they relate to students, adults or difficult situations we can often find ourselves in within the typical life of a school – and helping me find ways of resolving them intelligently. He has the knack of being able to separate salient points, boil issues down to their bare essentials and look practically and rationally at what constitutes success. His understanding of the relationship between behaviour, emotion, and cognition on the one hand, and brain function on the other, and his ability to share that understanding with others in a very practical way, has helped my staff develop their skills to be more effective when working with each other and students.

In short, he has a finely tuned ability to see right into your very soul!

There is not a better time for his approach to be fully understood by people wishing to make an impact on the growing issues relating to mental health and relationships. As a keen advocate of emotional intelligence in the workplace, for staff, students and parents, I find myself remarkably attuned to his way of thinking, analysing and strategically planning to move forward with my aims and values.

I know this work will appeal massively to any professional who shares an ambition to drive forward towards success in a completely human manner.

Jonny Mitchell
Principal, The Co-operative Academy of Leeds
#attendancematters

Jonny Mitchell was the head teacher of Thornhill Community Academy, which featured in Channel 4's series Educating Yorkshire. *He is now headteacher of The Co-operative Academy of Leeds. You can follow Jonny Mitchell on Twitter @MrMitchellCAL.*

Meet the author

Victor Allen, behaviour consultant, specialising in emotional intelligence and mental security. *'A keen advocate of the development of social and emotional intelligence for staff and students within the school setting.'*

For the past 15 years, Victor has worked as a freelance consultant in the educational, charitable and business sector, dealing with behaviour and leadership issues. He advises and teaches on improving all aspects of emotional and social intelligence with both staff and students. He is also a regular keynote speaker for conferences on aspects of mental security, whole school approaches to behaviour, and understanding the maturation of the brain.

Within the educational sector, he mentors and coaches head teachers, and middle and aspiring leaders as they develop their leadership skills and deal with difficult situations.

He coaches and mentors trainee teachers and NQTs in a variety of schools and universities, and also provides support and supervision for all members of staff within schools.

During the last two years he has created and developed a mental security programme which is being used to assist in the building of social and emotional resilience and coping strategies for students in primary, secondary, independent and special schools.

He also worked with the Queen's Trust for two years, supporting the CEOs and staff of some of the major charities supported by the Queen.

Introduction

This second edition seeks to meet the needs of teachers as they deal with a generation of students born in a different century to them. We know that significant changes and development take place within the brains of children during their early years. The start of early adolescence from the age of eight should also be taken into account, so with this in mind I have included within this book strategies for dealing with children in primary school. Over the years my work has developed and now includes regular visits to primary schools, so I thought it important to add some discussion of younger-age children to the book.

The whole landscape of childhood, education, work, play and health has radically changed, yet the instructions for teachers on how to manage classrooms have stayed relatively the same. Those of us who work within the educational system know that it is often used as a political tool to promote one idea over another and to bring changes that often seem to show little regard to the situations and reality within the classroom.

In the chapters that follow I will highlight what teachers can do within the classroom, as well as within schools, to provide those three basic psychological needs: a sense of Belonging, for them to exercise and have Autonomy within their lives and to grow positive Self-Esteem. Providing this solid BASE for students is not only needed but vital in order to counter the rising issues of mental health problems with students and the stress that this invariably brings to teachers and support staff within the school system.

Jonny Mitchell, who kindly wrote the endorsement for the book, was on television again recently, this time because his school in Leeds includes children from 72 different nationalities. The emotional, cultural and academic issues this brings to teachers all need to be taken into account. What I aim to highlight in this book is that with a solid BASE these things can be worked through. But that BASE has to come first for the brain to be educated well.

Therefore, this book aims to equip teachers with an understanding of what's going on in the minds of those they seek to teach. Even though the world may have changed, the maturation of the brain and the three basic psychological needs essential for human growth and development have not.

Equipping our students to meet the demands of this ever-changing world is also becoming the task of teachers; for some, their teacher may be the most stable, consistent and informative person they encounter in their daily life. One estimate suggests that 65% of children entering primary school today will ultimately end up working in completely new job types that aren't even on our radar yet. The most in-demand occupations did not exist 10 or even 5 years ago, and this pace of change is set to accelerate (for more information on this, go to www3.weforum.org/docs/WEF_ASEAN_HumanCapitalOutlook.pdf).

What is needed is for students to able to be mentally secure and emotionally and socially intelligent enough to meet this uncertain future so as to make the most of the new opportunities that will present themselves.

My good friend Dr Dietmar Seehuber has continued to advise and highlight new understanding of brain function, maturation and development. His work as a senior psychiatrist and psychotherapist, first in a children's hospital and now working with adults in a hospital just outside Frankfurt, means he is well placed to see first-hand when things don't go right. His work informs much of the thinking in this book.

I will touch on some of the aspects of brain maturation that I hope will encourage more study for those who are interested. It is vital that we recognise that children, from reception through to their leaving to go to employment, college or university, go through different stages, and it is also vital that we work with those changes.

I have brought together insights from my experience of working with young people and adults over the past 20 years or so – from persistent young offenders in inner-city Birmingham to excluded pupils from secondary schools, to those wanting to develop leadership schools in some of England's independent schools. I have listened to what motivates, scares or challenges them and also what annoys them as they seek to map out their own lives and future.

I hope that you find the book interesting and helpful. Dyslexia and writing books is never a good mixture, so I would like to acknowledge the ready assistance of Helen Fairlie, who has guided me so well in the process, as well as the publishers of this book who recognise the merit of educating the educators. Thank you for your patience with me. I would also like to thank the teachers who have tried some of the strategies that I suggest and shared their outcomes. The world is a better place through those who seek to teach well. I wish you, the reader, well and may your patience always be with you.

1 Where are we now and how have we got here?

Understanding the culture

This book enters a climate in which the focus on behaviour and the attainment of results (almost regardless of the social, economic and emotional background of our students) is high on the agenda of everyone with a vested interest in education – the government, local authorities, academy sponsors, etc. Working in a learning environment, you will be all too aware of how the attainment of outstanding behaviour and subsequent results are strong motivating factors for decisions being made in the world of education.

This first chapter explores the importance of understanding the unique culture into which you, as an educator, are entering and why some types of perceived poor behaviour emerge in the classroom. It is aimed at helping you use this knowledge to develop your practice in an environment where you will be expected to achieve the highest standards possible, while being constantly assessed by your peers, your faculty, your school leadership team, your students and their parents; as well as by external assessors, including the local authority and Ofsted itself.

Challenging behaviour

Defining poor behaviour is not straightforward and there are many differing definitions (Department for Education, 2012). However, it is very clear that the many perceived aspects of 'poor behaviour' continue to influence learning in the classroom.

The Programme for International Student Assessment (PISA) results reflect the existence of disruption in classrooms – eg 31 per cent of pupils in England felt that *'in most or all lessons'* that *'there is noise and disorder'* (Bradshaw et al, 2010).

The Teaching and Learning International Survey (TALIS, 2013) reported that, in most of the 23 countries surveyed, up to 25 per cent of teachers lost at least 30 per cent of their lesson time to disruptions as well as administrative tasks. An international average of 13 per cent of teacher time is reportedly spent on maintaining order in the classroom (OECD, 2010).

Her Majesty's Chief Inspector (HMCI) raised concerns about low-level disruption in schools in his Annual Report 2012/13 (Ofsted, 2013). As a consequence, guidance to inspectors was tightened to place greater emphasis on this issue in routine inspections. In addition, HMCI commissioned a survey to ascertain the nature and extent of low-level disruptive behaviour in primary and secondary schools in England (Ofsted, 2014). The survey includes some teachers' comments on the disruptive behaviour issues they face (Ofsted, 2014, p 47):

> *Talking to each other (not about the work); texting or looking at mobile phones; rocking on chair or getting up from seat; putting on make-up; messing about with friends – for example play-fighting; dropping pens and equipment on the floor; throwing paper planes.*
>
> Secondary school teacher
>
> *Talking to classmates when the teacher is talking; calling out answers instead of raising a hand; making silly comments for attention; passing notes; surreptitious*

throwing of small pieces of paper; arriving late to lessons; deliberately sitting in the wrong seat; minor squabbles during group work tasks.

Primary school teacher

Chatting; not working; not focusing on the task set, just sitting there doing nothing; uniform incorrect, including wearing make-up; rolling eyes at teachers or other impolite gestures or behaviours; lack of homework, making it difficult to continue with your scheme of learning; calling out; demanding attention without regard for other students' needs; refusing or delaying with argument [about] taking off of coats and not placing bags on the floor; turning up late, disrupting the learning going on in the lesson.

Secondary school teacher

Children talking between themselves when they should be listening; fiddling with anything; writing when they should be listening; refusing to work with a talk partner.

Primary school teacher

This is behaviour is not just confined to England. A YouGov poll found 57% of teachers in Wales had reported worsening behaviour – above the UK average of 49% – and more than a third (34%) had considered leaving the profession as a result (Education Support Partnership, 2014).

Two thirds (66%) of teachers surveyed in Wales said that poor behaviour had resulted in stress, anxiety or depression (Evans, 2014).

The Educational Institute of Scotland (EIS) found that the majority of pupils are normally well behaved, but that a 'persistent minority' often fail to behave appropriately (Johnson, 2015).

In Northern Ireland, the NASUWT report that teachers believe that there is a widespread problem with pupil behaviour in schools today. Teachers cannot teach, and pupils cannot learn in an environment where there is disruption and violence. 42% believe that there is a pupil behaviour problem in their school. 80% believe that there is an issue of low-level disruptive behaviour among the pupils they teach (NASUWT, nd).

It is therefore vitally important for you to gain as much understanding as possible about the young people you are going to teach, so that you are fully equipped to avoid disruptions and challenges to your authority within your classroom and the wider school environment. This will almost certainly require knowledge about your students' academic ability, but it also involves acquiring as much information as possible about the stages of social, physical and mental growth they have reached and their related impact.

Setting the scene

Our brains have evolved over 200,000 years, and include inherited personal characteristics that have been genetically handed down to us through generations.

We are hardwired to react to stress in a specific way that prepares us for life and death situations – this is what faced us as human beings for thousands of years as we found ourselves in the middle of the food chain. Wild animals react to us now in the same way we would have reacted to things on a daily basis; there had to be constant vigilance to check and react to anything that had the potential to kill. Eventually, through our own manipulation of resources, we moved to the top of the food chain, yet our reactions have not made as rapid a change. So when we encounter things that cause us uncertainty and stress, that seem unfamiliar or cause us anxiety, we often overreact as if we again are in a situation that evokes the fight or flight response. Emotional intelligence helps us to counter that hard-wired process we still automatically turn to.

Your students are growing up in an ever changing world. They have been influenced by their social surroundings and the people they have met as well as the wide-ranging media, social networking and interactive games that increasingly demand their attention.

The landscape in which young people learn social and emotional intelligence to equip them to grow as fully functioning social individuals has changed. Children growing up today now have ready access to foods containing high levels of sugar, and the easy availability of digital technologies (television, mobile phones, tablets, computer games, etc) tends to contribute to disrupted sleeping patterns. I believe that this has led to the rise in mental health issues among children, as well as their increasing lack of concentration and social engagement within class and at school in general.

All these influences will be brought into your classroom, where they will affect each individual's behaviour – how they cope with the information and instructions you provide, how they perceive the way in which you communicate, how they interact with their peers, how they handle the stresses and pressures of education.

The classroom is, quite simply, one of the most important life-developing environments in which we place young people today. It will influence them for the rest of their lives, teaching them what they are capable of, helping them discover their interests and laying the foundation for what they believe they can and can't do.

In a timely study at the end of the last century (Connell and Wellborn, 1991), which looked at the need for belonging in the school community, researchers found that the support relationship with adults in school had more effect on students' psychological state than support from home.

The behaviour of students in your classroom has to be at least good, in order to ensure this learning time is as beneficial as possible. How can you guarantee this is the case?

It is your responsibility, as an educator, to know and recognise these influences, and to be fully aware of their impact on the success of your students and, indeed, your future teaching career.

This book draws upon my experiences over the last 25 years as a behaviour consultant within both the educational and business sectors, encouraging groups to examine their practice, as they aspire to be the best they can possibly be and function effectively as teams as well as individuals.

It also focuses on the advancements in neuroscience over the last 20 years in relation to MRI (magnetic resonance imaging) and functional magnetic resonance imaging (functional MRI, fMRI), and how this information can help make sense of young people and the changes they are undergoing through adolescence.

Ongoing perceptions

It is nothing new to attribute young people's poor and disruptive behaviour to the evolvement of a *'new generation of badly behaved and ill-disciplined children'*. The passage below, often attributed to Socrates, is worth considering

> *The children now love luxury; they have bad manners, contempt for authority; they show disrespect for elders and love chatter in place of exercise. Children are now tyrants, not the servants of their households. They no longer rise when elders enter the room. They contradict their parents, chatter before company, gobble up dainties at the table, cross their legs, and tyrannize their teachers.*
>
> Socrates, fifth century BC

Whoever the author, the message is familiar and it is clearly an old one. Adults do have difficulty in trying to understand and manage the changes young people go through and the perceived disruption they cause, and this has been true throughout the generations.

With every new cohort of young people, it is therefore necessary to understand the challenges that are current, in order to address them as effectively as possible.

Justifying an opposition to learning

During the Thatcher years, an insufficiently motivating curriculum was beginning to be blamed for students' lack of interest in learning and a reluctance to engage in teachers' learning strategies. This was to be addressed by the introduction of the national curriculum.

These days, a credible reason is the perceived erosion of boundaries that young people experience as they grow up. Michele Elliott of the children's charity Kidscape said: *'Children no longer have boundaries. It's bad for children and it's bad for parents. Some parents, due to a lack of time, pressures at work and so forth, are trying to buy their children's love, which is toxic'* (quoted in the *Daily Mail*, 14 September 2009: www.dailymail.co.uk/news/article-1213236/The-spoilt-generation-Youngsters-lack-respect-authority-attacking-parents-police-teachers.html).

Teachers Under Pressure, a report published by Cambridge University's Faculty of Education in 2008, identified a growing trend of disobedience at home spilling into classrooms, highlighting *'highly permissive parenting and misguided discipline policies in school resulting in poor pupil behaviour reaching the highest levels'* (Galton, 2008). These children, in their teens then, could well be the parents of the generations entering school now, which could also help explain the lack of parenting skills that is in evidence today.

More recent recognition

We are all now far more accepting of the notion that teenagers go through a period of upheaval caused by fluctuating hormones. Discoveries through MRI scans have highlighted that a teenager's brain is transforming through a developmental process, contradicting the earlier assumption that the brain is fully developed during early childhood (see Chapter 2).

It would be wrong to suggest that understanding the development of the brain during this period holds all the answers, but it should be placed alongside our accepted knowledge of the growth and development of young people.

As the frontal lobes of the brain (sometimes referred to as the higher brain) are not fully mature until a person is in their early twenties, your students will almost definitely have difficulties in managing emotions appropriately as they progress through the changes from being dependent children into independent adults.

We know that early experiences can have great potential to affect brain development. Children are especially vulnerable to persistent negative input, yet these years are also a great opportunity for teachers to provide positive experiences that can have a huge effect on children's mental wellbeing as they grow towards adulthood.

Early adolescence starts around the ages of eight or nine, when a child starts to move from being a child towards becoming an adult. They are thus beginning a journey away from the rules and constraints of adults as they seek independence. This is also a time for them to experiment and rebel as they search for their own identity, and it's important for us not to see these stages as a challenge to our authority but a normal process they are going through.

It is therefore important to be equipped to support your students in managing appropriate thoughts and actions. How often have you tried to use reason and logic to encourage a student to make a positive choice when, in fact, their brain hasn't engaged the under-developed frontal area necessary for judgement, logic or planning? Instead, this has been hijacked by the more fully advanced emotional areas which are then used, almost exclusively, to make decisions and initiate actions.

Firmer discipline?

There are a number of people who feel very strongly that they understand how to address poor behaviour.

A recent poll conducted by YouGov researchers and commissioned by the *Times Educational Supplement* polled 2,014 parents with children at secondary school and 530 secondary-age pupils between 19 and 30 August 2012.

> *While significant numbers favoured corporal punishment, sending pupils out of the class was the most popular method of dealing with indiscipline, chosen by 89 per cent of parents and 79 per cent of children.*

Other popular ways of cracking down on bad behaviour were lunchtime or after-school detentions and writing lines.

More than four in five parents (84 per cent) and nearly two thirds of children (62 per cent) backed expelling or suspending naughty pupils.

(Loveys, 2011)

It is most probably a fear that behaviour in schools is worse than it has been in previous years that drives some to think punishment is a motivating factor in the improvement of behaviour.

However, those actually working within education are fully aware that simply issuing detentions or excluding pupils may have an impact on a few students, but will most definitely not be the changing factor for those determined to misbehave.

Alternative approaches are needed to support students in making better choices for themselves and in working with, rather than against, those trying to support them.

Firmer discipline and sanctions are the last things that some of the teenagers and young people need. Research from the United States shows that in 2016, an estimated 2.2 million adolescents aged 12 to 17 in the US had at least one major depressive episode with severe impairment. This number represented 9% of the US population aged 12 to 17 (NIMH, 2018).

You will see that building resilience is for some an answer to helping young people cope with the problems that life will inevitably bring. I agree that is important that we do so, and that this should be coupled with building excellent relationships with those who come to your school.

Begin at the beginning

To ensure you can establish a relationship with your students that guides them through the emotional traumas of school and life itself and allows them to achieve their full potential and build resilience, it is necessary to start at the beginning and examine the experiences of young people in today's world.

Childhood play

The brain is continually learning, and trial and error, as well as watching and listening to others, is fundamental in the process of developing a whole range of social, cognitive, attention, memory, language, reasoning, problem-solving and decision-making skills.

Childhood play, therefore, and particularly unstructured play, is a vital influence on personal development.

Learning through play

'Learning through play' is used by both educationalists and psychologists to describe how children develop the skills described above, particularly through unstructured play, when the imagination is used and developed. In such play, children develop the self-confidence required to engage in new experiences and tasks.

In the book *Einstein Never Used Flash Cards* (Hirsh-Pasek and Michnick Golinkoff, 2003), five elements of children's play are defined.

1.   Play must be pleasurable and enjoyable.

2.   Play must have no extrinsic goals; there is no prescribed learning that must occur.

3.   Play is spontaneous and voluntary.

4.   Play involves active engagement on the part of the player.

5.   Play involves an element of make-believe.

Quite simply, play enables children to learn to make sense of their world. It should never be viewed as a waste of time, but rather a phase of building upon previous learning and expanding the very ability a child needs to cope with the society in which they are going to play a role.

The theorist John Dewey suggests that children learn best by both physical and intellectual activity. In other words, children need to take an active role in play.

Changes in childhood play

One of the biggest changes that has taken place over the last 20 years is the way children now spend their free time and interact with each other. Below is an extract from an e-mail that was circulating the web. It is referring to children who were born in the 1950s and 60s.

WE WERE ALWAYS OUTSIDE PLAYING!!

We would leave home in the morning and play all day, as long as we were back when the streetlights came on.

No one was able to reach us all day. And we were OK.

We would spend hours building our go-carts out of scraps and then ride down the hill, only to find out we forgot the brakes. After running into the bushes a few times, we learned to solve the problem.

We did not have Playstations, Nintendos, Xboxes, Wii, no video games at all, no 99 channels, no Pay TV, no Sky, no DVD movies or surround sound.

It's crazy! There were no mobile phones, no text messaging, no personal computers, no Internet or Internet chat rooms...

WE HAD FRIENDS and we went outside and found them!

We fell out of trees, got cut, broke bones and teeth and there were no lawsuits from these accidents.

We played with worms and mud pies made from dirt, and the worms did not live in us forever.

Made up games with sticks and tennis balls and although we were told it would happen, we didn't poke out anyone's eye.

We rode bikes or walked to a friend's house and knocked on the door or rang the bell, or just yelled for them!

Local teams had try-outs and not everyone made the team. Those who didn't had to learn to deal with disappointment. Imagine that!!

The idea of a parent bailing us out if we broke the law was unheard of. They actually sided with the law!

We had freedom, failure, success and responsibility, and we learned how to deal with it all!

Critical questions

» *What competencies relevant to adult life were being developed here?*

» *Can you identify the development of independence, communication skills, self- and social responsibility, initiative and motivation, to name but a few?*

» *In addition, consider the development of self-confidence, trustworthiness and imaginative skills, all in the absence of adult supervision or a formal learning environment.*

» *Would there have been a difference in the impact on learning if an adult had been present?*

At this point, it is worth considering where our young people have the opportunity to develop these competencies today.

Play in the twenty-first century

The advent of personal computers, electronic games and instant communication is one obvious contributing factor to changes in childhood play today.

The first text message was sent on the 3 December 1992, when a 22-year-old British engineer, Neil Papworth, used his computer to wish a Merry Christmas to Richard Jarvis of Vodafone on his mobile phone. By the year 2001, the UK was sending one billion texts a month. In 2012, Ofcom reported that text messages were now the most frequently used method for daily communication with family and friends.

Sitting in front of a screen has begun to take the place of childhood unstructured play when, in previous generations, children learnt how to interact with others, developing social skills and imagination.

Further effects of new technologies on the developing brain

Enthusiasm for the advantages offered by screen technology is generally more pronounced when considering the use of computers in schools, yet there are a number of large, well-controlled studies that fail to support this presumption. For example, a study of 15-year-old students in 31 countries concluded that those using computers at school several times a week performed *'sizeably and statistically significantly worse'* in both mathematics and reading than those who used them less often (Fuchs and Wössmann, 2004). Another study from Duke University, involving 150,000 pupils aged 10 to 14, compared the same children's reading and mathematics scores before and after they acquired a home computer. Researchers also compared the scores of peers who had always had a home computer with those who had never had access to one. Findings suggested that providing children with regular access to a computer could actually hinder their reading and mathematics skills – *'the introduction of home computer technology is associated with statistically significant and persistent negative impacts on student math and reading test scores'* (Vigdor and Ladd, 2010).

Researcher Jacob Vigdor concluded that, for schools hoping to maximise attainment or reduce the impact of socio-economic disparities, *'a programme of broadening home computer access would be counter-productive'*.

It would be wrong to think it is simply children sitting in front of screens all day that results in social and emotional developmental problems, and it probably needs to be recognised that absolutely anything that distracts a child from being involved in unstructured play will also be preventing opportunities for learning as children are intended to learn.

There is little doubt that the internet and screen time are having an impact on the way children learn as well as their brain development. As the technology writer Nicholas Carr has observed (Carr, 2010), the emergence of reading encouraged our brains to be focused and imaginative. In contrast, the rise of the internet is strengthening our ability to scan information rapidly and efficiently. Technology conditions the brain to pay attention to information in very different ways to reading a book.

The focus on academic development

There is tremendous pressure on parents to raise their children to have the best possible start in life, but this is often perceived as ensuring their children are studying and learning things that will give them a head start in school on an academic front, with attainment of examination results as the ultimate goal.

However, it is clear that, alongside this rational part of our brain, it is the emotional mind that will be relied upon to guide actions and choices throughout life and will often spring into action far more quickly than our rational thoughts.

How often have you found yourself reacting emotionally to an event and then, later reflecting that this was not the best course of action?

It is unstructured play – watching and interacting with others, learning from mistakes and learning to choose courses and outcomes – that is productive, rather than destructive, and that is mainly responsible for this absolutely vital area of emotional development that supports academic learning at school.

Emotional intelligence

Daniel Goleman, in his book *Emotional Intelligence: Why It Can Matter More Than IQ* (2005), made it clear that an emotionally intelligent person is far more likely to succeed within their chosen career and handle the daily pressures of life than someone who struggles to manage their emotions.

What is emotional intelligence?

Goleman listed five competencies in relation to emotional intelligence. These are:

1. knowing one's own emotions – self-awareness, having an ability to recognise one's own feelings and why someone feels as they do;

2. managing emotions – being able to take control and manage emotions, for example, controlling anger;

3. motivating oneself;

4. recognising emotions in others – considering how others feel and responding appropriately towards them;

5. handling relationships – the ability to make friends and keep them, demonstrating competent leadership, coping with differences in others.

Emotional intelligence is, therefore, the ability to understand one's own emotions and those of others, and to use this understanding and information to ensure the very best outcomes for all concerned. It also means being able to acknowledge where these emotions come from, what triggers them and how best to manage them.

This intelligence will enable a person to work well on their own as well as with others, because it provides the foundation upon which the cognitive part of the brain can be used to its fullest extent. It is this emotional intelligence that drives the rational mind.

Although these skills will most definitely continue to be learnt and developed throughout life, it is very important for them to have a foundation laid down in early years through experiences of, for example, unstructured play and interacting emotionally with others.

Government awareness

By the late 1990s, the government was being made aware, through representatives from industry as well as numerous other sources, that standards of emotional maturity among graduates and other young people, as well as the use of initiative, had fallen to significantly low levels.

It was during this time that I distinctly remember delivering a development training session for a group of HSBC fast-track managers, through team-building and problem-solving exercises. The lack of understanding in relation to team dynamics, alongside the absence of initiative and empathy, was extremely evident within this group of highly academic and competent people.

Each individual was considered to have a fabulous potential within HSBC, after having succeeded in a particularly stringent selection process. Yet there was an absence of some of the most basic skills required to manage and lead others.

In recognising a need for the development of social and emotional skills, the government introduced the notion of social emotional learning (SEL) into schools. From 2000, personal, social, health and economic (PSHE) education, in a variety of forms, became part of the national curriculum, described by Ofsted as a planned programme to help children and young people develop fully as individuals and as members of families and social and economic communities. Its goal was to equip young people with the knowledge, understanding, attitudes and practical skills to live healthily, safely, productively and responsibly.

In addition to this, there has been a sustained focus on the social and emotional aspects of learning (SEAL) in schools.

One size doesn't fit all

Teaching the competencies of emotional intelligence within classroom environments has had limited success. Unfortunately, but perhaps not surprisingly, research in both America and the UK has noted that prescriptive 'one-size-fits-all' approaches such as SEAL can, in fact, be counterproductive.

The government's recently published conclusions following a review of SEAL within schools noted:

> *Finally, in terms of impact, our analysis of pupil-level outcome data indicated that SEAL (as implemented by schools in our sample) failed to impact significantly upon pupils' social and emotional skills, general mental health difficulties, pro-social behaviour or behaviour problems. And analysis of school climate scores indicated significant reductions in pupils' trust and respect for teachers, liking for school, and feelings of classroom and school supportiveness during SEAL implementation. Additionally, qualitative data around perceptions of impact indicated a feeling that SEAL had not produced the expected changes across schools.*
>
> (Department for Education, 2010)

Current focus

The Ofsted Common Inspection Framework (2015) states that:

> *Inspectors will evaluate the extent to which the school successfully promotes and supports pupils'*
>
> • *employability skills so that they are well prepared for the next stage of their education, employment, self-employment or training;*

- *understanding of how to keep themselves safe from relevant risks such as abuse, sexual exploitation and extremism, including when using the internet and social media;*
- *knowledge of how to keep themselves healthy, both emotionally and physically, including through exercising and healthy eating;*
- *personal development, so that they are well prepared to respect others and contribute to wider society and life in Britain.*

(Ofsted, 2015, p 14)

In response to this, there has to be a whole-school ethos, interwoven through lessons, that promotes students becoming self-assured, confident, happy and positive young people who are continuously developing personal self-knowledge.

I have written a Mental Security Program which will be explained later in the book. This covers the key foundational requirement needed for the cognitive development of young people and students.

CASE STUDY

Whitley Academy

I was first introduced to Victor when our Principal invited him in after seeing him present at a Secondary Headteachers conference and being inspired by Victor's visionary approach to emotional intelligence in schools.

Victor initially met with our senior leadership group and talked to us about 'The 3 Ms' and the importance of giving each child a sense of belonging, autonomy and self-esteem in order to enable them to achieve self-actualisation. It was so refreshing to listen to Victor talk about something I'm so passionate about with such clarity. I was really excited at the prospect of working collaboratively with someone with such a deep understanding and proven track record in this field, as for the first time we had a real opportunity to fully embed a culture of emotional intelligence and mental security within Whitley Academy (which is something we have been working towards for many years but never fully realised in a 'whole-school' sense).

Victor has led on two whole-school inset training days and has enabled all staff to look at building mental security through 'fresh eyes' as part of creating the culture we want. All staff now have a good understanding of how words can harm or heal, why all students and staff need to feel they are valued and belong, and the importance of making everything we do meaningful. We have run assemblies on emotional intelligence with all year groups (7–11) using Victor's age-appropriate materials, and have delivered Victor's scheme of work on mental security to the whole of Year 9 through weekly tutor-time sessions. We targeted this year group as this stage of adolescence tends to be the most challenging time of their school careers for many of our students emotionally and behaviourally. Year on year we experience higher numbers of fixed-term exclusions in Year 9 comparatively with other year groups.

Historically we have somewhat naively put this down to 'hormones', but Victor's insightful training around brain development has given staff a new empathy and understanding, which has triggered a new approach with our Year 9s. To complement the tutor-time sessions, we also started to deliver a 'Mental Security' unit within our carousel lessons, which is a programme of work which runs for six weeks with every class in Year 9.

The students' feedback was that they really enjoyed the course, and we have therefore rolled this out with all of Year 7 and 8 as part of their citizenship curriculum. Again, the feedback has been really encouraging and we are looking to embed this within the Key Stage 4 curriculum next year. Additionally, we ran a whole-school 'Mental Security' day recently, during which all pupils in all year groups had mental-health-themed lessons (again, using some of Victor's outstanding lesson plans), circle time and/or workshops related to emotional intelligence. Outside of the classroom we have developed a working party of 'Mental Security Champions' who have met regularly to create a vision statement for the school, lead on emotional-intelligence/mental-security initiatives with students and families, and role-model the principles of the 3 Ms to newer staff to help embed the approach.

The impact of all of this (thanks to Victor's guidance, support and ideas) has been a significant shift in the behaviour of students in Key Stage 3, especially with our Year 9 cohort where there has been more intense targeted intervention. The number of fixed-term exclusions in this year group has reduced noticeably. Student–staff and staff–staff relationships have improved. Interestingly, whole-school attendance is increasing due to internal truancy diminishing. We would argue that is in part due to front-line teachers continually looking for opportunities to give students that sense of belonging that they so desperately need, and now those children who might in the past have been called 'corridor kids' are very rarely sent out of lessons.

We are about to embark on the second year of our Mental Security journey and I am so excited about how much more can be achieved in the future. Moving forward at Whitley Academy, Mental Security is going to be a priority within the Whole-School Improvement Plan as well as being included in all departmental Linked Improvement Plans. This ensures that all staff, in spite of career stage or role, play their part in embedding emotional intelligence year on year.

On a more personal note, working with Victor has been a breath of fresh air for me. My background being in SEMH (social emotional and mental health) and Inclusion, Victor's approach is 'right up my street' so to speak! His expertise, insight and supportive nature has really helped me to drive this agenda forward at Whitley Academy, as well as helping me to develop professionally and reigniting my passion through coaching.

Reality check

It has to be remembered that for 200,000 years, human beings have grown up learning, through experience, the necessary skills to become active members of society. This has been achieved without constructed, specifically related lessons, but through interaction with one another and understanding the part we all play in the well-being of others as well as ourselves. Humans have had to learn that life isn't always fair, isn't always nice and we can't win and succeed all the time. When we get knocked down or knocked back, or have to face things we fear or don't like, the best way to do so is to tackle them head on, rather than trying to avoid or ignore them or look to others to deal with them for us. We recognise that people we meet might be different from us, but we have to learn to get along with them. We make friends and find partners and have to learn to make a success of situations that aren't always easy.

We learn there are some people we can rely on and others we can't. We learn that some are cruel and others will be supportive and loving. We learn that some things are in our control, while others are not.

All of our experiences are unique, because we view them though our personal perspective and understanding. But it is developing this emotional and social intelligence that makes us who we are.

Young people, adolescence and independence

As young people begin learning to take control of their lives and become independent, they often struggle with an overload of emotions, driven by hormones and physical changes. The front part of their brain is trying to make sense of the world and establish some sort of order.

It is only when the competencies as described earlier eventually become the norm that we recognise an emotionally intelligent person. This has to be a personal journey that each individual travels through.

It is absolutely essential that you as educators and other adults recognise the part you can play in supporting youngsters as they experience this transition.

In his blog 'Surviving your child's adolescence', Carl Pickhardt (2018) explains:

> The birth of the 'bad attitude' begins in early adolescence because people do not change unless they are dissatisfied with who and how they are. And the early adolescent is developmentally dissatisfied. He doesn't want to be defined and treated as a child any more.

Your students' development in relation to the competencies

During my training sessions, I ask teachers to look at the list of competencies described earlier and make a judgement about to what extent their students demonstrate them on a regular basis.

It is usually clear that the vast majority of young people find it difficult to manage more than one of the competencies at any given time.

In fact, I am sure you also know a few adults who are still struggling to master this.

It's important to understand that, during this time, when the front part of the brain is learning to master emotions, plan and think ahead through experiences and contact with others (see Chapter 2), many young people are unfortunately spending time in activities that actually avoid contact with others. They are also too readily seeking out adults to solve any emotional problems they encounter.

Adult assistance

In schools, I constantly see and hear subject teachers, form tutors and support staff address-ing difficulties between students that, in the past, would never have been brought to the attention of an adult but would have been sorted out by the children themselves. The amount of time spent by adults dealing with issues in relation to the breakdown of friendships and low-level comments made by one about another is on the increase.

I'm not referring to 'sorting it out' through a full-scale argument or degeneration into a fight. Young people would very often have found an appropriate solution themselves by talking things through, looking for compromises, seeking clarity of the situation to aid understanding or simply choosing to look to other friends for support.

Today's challenges for young people in dealing with friendship and relationship issues pose a responsibility for teachers and others in education not to be the solver but to be a coach in developing students' knowledge and skills in resolving problems for themselves.

Your advice to students

I always advise teachers, when presented with a relatively minor issue by a student, to first ask what three actions or attempts the student has taken themselves to attempt to resolve the problem. Telling an adult should not be considered one of the strategies!

Over time, young people will get used to only approaching you for help once they have made attempts to solve their problem themselves. This places you in a far better position to help students discuss these approaches and then reflect on 'next steps'.

Ideally, and with developed knowledge and skills, problems will begin to be addressed through the students' initial attempts and strategies and without needing your expert input.

Wider issues

This chapter has referred to a number of influences on the development of teenagers that have been emerging over the last 15 years.

A recent UNICEF report on the lives and well-being of children and adolescents in all economically advanced nations indicates that the main barrier to child well-being in the UK is family breakdown. For many young people, the break-up of adult relationships is the norm.

The report also noted families in OECD countries being aware of the reshaping of childhood as a result of forces whose mainspring is not necessarily the best interests of the child. This is alongside a growing awareness of the corrosive social problems affecting quality of life, with their genesis in the changing ecology of childhood.

Many therefore feel it is time to regain a degree of understanding, control and direction over what is happening to our children during their most vital, vulnerable years.

Challenges in relation to young people's well-being are the result of an enormous number of social and cultural changes, including:

- family breakdown;
- community breakdown;
- rise in drug and alcohol abuse;
- the impact of the mass media;
- advertising/marketing/higher expectations;
- pressure to achieve (exams, etc);
- materialism;
- increasing inequalities;
- decline in religion;
- lack of exercise;
- poor diet/eating habits/additives;
- pessimism of the age (eg ecological disasters).

An awareness of these issues will help you understand some of the context and situations your students are facing, feeling, thinking and worrying about.

As their teacher, you are then more equipped to support them in addressing these challenges in a clear and rational way, allowing you more easily to be not only their teacher of academic learning but also a coach in their overall emotional development.

Critical reflection

Entering into a working environment that has a dramatic impact on the academic, emotional and physical development of young people obviously requires you to be a subject specialist, but it also necessitates you taking on the role of an effective communicator, guide and leader.

Throughout your teaching career, you will be required to manage your own feelings and reflect on the academic but also the emotional outcomes of your lessons in terms of yourself and your students. This will be vital in terms of learning from your experiences and adjusting your teaching accordingly.

What is reflection?

In *Becoming a Critically Reflective Teacher*, Stephen Brookfield (1995) wrote that the goal was to develop an increased awareness of your teaching from as many different vantage points as possible.

Brookfield proposes four lenses that you can use in the process of critical reflection:

1. the autobiographical;
2. the students' eyes;
3. your colleagues' experiences;
4. the theoretical literature.

Examining each of these perspectives provides the foundation for good teaching and the means to become an excellent teacher.

You can build on the autobiographical focus, or self-reflection, by focusing on your previous experiences as a learner and on your experiences as a teacher. Don't limit your reflection to the academic aspect alone, but reflect on your personal and emotional development during your time with your students.

It is with this ability to reflect and develop the skills of an emotionally competent teacher that will support you in delivering relevant and life-changing experiences within your classroom.

CASE STUDY

During a lesson relating to the English Civil War, students had been reflecting on how propaganda literature was written with a bias towards the victors. The teacher identified an opportunity to encourage students to reflect on their relationships with each other and asked them to describe a time when someone had made up unpleasant stories about them. A group of girls were very keen to talk about their 'ex-friend', and did so with the emotional tone you might expect.

The teacher responded by commenting on the manner and vigour with which their views were being expressed.

The teacher then posed the question: *'Have you ever exaggerated something a brother, sister or friend has done to make it sound worse than it actually was?'*

A lively discussion ensued about what students had said to purposely *'get others into trouble'* as well as exaggerated stories they knew had been made up about themselves.

In summing up these reflections, the teacher asked her class to consider why individuals go to such lengths to contrive information about others to portray them in a bad light. Answers initially centred around: *'it's fun'*, *'to get others into trouble'*, *'to get my own back'*. This then developed into an understanding of selfish reasons and a desire to gain vengeance, etc, alongside alternative, more appropriate patterns of behaviour and actions.

Returning to the English Civil War, by reflecting on their own experiences, students were then more clearly able to consider the motives behind the propaganda and the subsequent effect on others.

This shift away from the initial lesson subject matter had allowed students to develop aspects of their emotional intelligence, not through being told what to think and do, but by being guided towards deciding themselves between less and more appropriate actions.

Not all learning situations provide such excellent openings, but seeking out opportunities such as this is facilitating emotional learning, without detracting from any academic learning intentions.

The impact of your own experiences

Later chapters focus on the development of your own emotional intelligence, alongside your leadership skills and qualities.

However, at this stage I ask you to reflect on your understanding of the impact your own upbringing has had upon you as the unique individual you are now.

Think about the things you consider important and why they are important to you. Where did the understanding of their importance come from?

It is so important to consider how you view your students and how you emotionally engage with them.

Critical questions

» *Think about the groups that you absolutely love teaching. Why is this the case? What characteristics do these students demonstrate and how does that relate to your personal experiences?*

» *Think about the students that you perhaps struggle a little more with and ask yourself the same questions.*

» *What emotional competencies are the first groups showing and what competencies are the second groups not showing?*

Now consider addressing the competencies you feel are lacking within the teaching groups you find most difficult.

This doesn't mean pointing it out and telling them.

Your students will need alternatives to consider, brought to their attention through reflective coaching and positive experiences.

Chapter reflections

» *Understanding the culture and climate of the education sector will help you prepare yourself as fully as possible to address the variety of issues that will undoubtedly arise as you strive to become an outstanding teacher.*

» *Comprehending and addressing teenage behaviour has been acknowledged as an ongoing dilemma over a number of generations.*

» *However, today's advances in sociology and psychiatry, alongside discoveries through MRI scans, have provided us with advanced knowledge and understanding. Recognition that the brain grows through specific developmental stages and only reaches maturity in an individual's early twenties has clear implications for your decisions and actions as a classroom teacher.*

» *Unstructured play is hugely important in emotional development and securing strategies to cope with life's challenges, yet, over the past 20 years, the nature of childhood activity has changed. New technologies have had a huge impact on the way in which young people communicate with each other and spend their leisure time.*

» *Parents' promotion of academic qualifications as the optimum foundation for their child's start in life could be disadvantaging the emotional development of young people.*

» *As young people enter into the world of employment, the implications of a lack of emotional intelligence have become apparent, leading to governments trying to compensate by initiating the specific teaching of emotional and social learning. This has had extremely limited impact.*

» *As educators, you are therefore faced with needing to more fully appreciate how to support this developmental need within your personal classroom environment.*

» *Your students will most probably actively seek your help as they attempt to cope with pressures within their lives and the pressures of society today. They may, alternatively, try to use inappropriate behaviour or other avoidance techniques instead of addressing situations they find difficult. Your skills of guiding, coaching and mentoring will be vital in encouraging the development of emotional competencies, as outlined earlier in this chapter.*

» *It is essential that you continually reflect on the emotional aspects of your lessons, as well as your subject-teaching skills, as you progress through your teaching career. This will ensure your achievement as an outstanding educator of young people, rather than simply a teacher of a specifically chosen subject area.*

Taking it further

This will provide you an insight to the popular idea towards the return of corporal punishment within schools: www.dailymail.co.uk/news/article-2038030/Bring-cane-say-half-parents-Cameron-pledges-restore-order-schools-following-riots.html#ixzz2DifAsoKs

References

Association of Teachers and Lecturers (2012) *A Third of Education Staff Have Dealt with Physical Violence from Pupils in This School Year, with Parents Failing to Back Schools*. ATL press release. London: ATL. [online] Available at: www.atl.org.uk/latest/press-release/third-education-staff-have-dealt-physical-violence-pupils-school-year-parents (last accessed 26 May 2018).

Bradshaw, J, Ager, R, Burge, B and Wheater, R (2010) *PISA 2009: Achievement of 15-year-olds in England*. Slough: NFER.

Brookfield, S (1995) *Becoming a Critically Reflective Teacher*. San Francisco, CA: Jossey-Bass.

Carr, N (2010) The Web Shatters Focus, Rewires Brains. [online] Available at: www.wired.com/magazine/2010/05/ff_nicholas_carr/all/1 (last accessed 24 May 2018).

Connell, J and Wellborn, J (1991) Competence, Autonomy, and Relatedness: A Motivational Analysis of Self-System Processes. *Journal of Personality and Social Psychology*, 65.

Department for Education (2010) *Social and Emotional Aspects of Learning (SEAL) Programme in Secondary Schools: National Evaluation*. Research Report DFE-RR049.

Department for Education (2012) *Pupil Behaviour in Schools in England*. Research Report DFE-RR218 *Pupil Behaviour in Schools in England*. [online] Available at: www.gov.uk/government/publications/pupil-behaviour-in-schools-in-england (last accessed 26 May 2018).

Education Support Partnership (2014) Behaviour Survey. [online] Available at: www.educationsupport partnership.org.uk/resources/research-reports/behaviour-survey (last accessed 25 May 2018).

Evans, G (2014) Decline in Pupil Behaviour is an Increasing Problem for Teachers. Wales Online. [online] Available at: www.walesonline.co.uk/news/wales-news/decline-pupil-behaviour-issue-teachers-6708231 (last accessed 25 May 2018).

Fuchs, T and Wössmann, L (2004) Computers and Student Learning: Bivariate and Multivariate Evidence on the Availability and Use of Computers At Home and At School. *Brussels Economic Review*, 47(3–4): 359–86.

Galton, M (2008) Teachers Under Pressure: The Impact of Government Policies on Teachers' Working Lives. *Education Review* 21(1): 39–48.

Goleman, D (2005) *Emotional Intelligence: Why It Can Matter More Than IQ*. New York: Bantam Books.

Hirsh-Pasek, K and Michnick Golinkoff, R (2003) *Einstein Never Used Flash Cards*, Emmaus, PA: Rodale.

Johnson, S (2015) Teacher Cuts Blamed for Bad Behaviour in Scottish Schools. *Telegraph*. [online] Available at: www.telegraph.co.uk/news/uknews/scotland/11322016/Teacher-cuts-blamed-for-bad-behaviour-in-Scottish-schools.html (last accessed 25 May 2018).

Loveys, K (2011) Bring Back the Cane, Say Half of Parents as Cameron Pledges to Restore Order in Schools Following Riots. *Daily Mail*, 16 September. [online] Available at: www.dailymail.co.uk/news/article-2038030/Bring-cane-say-half-parents-Cameron-pledges-restore-order-schools-following-riots.html#ixzz2DifAsoKs (last accessed 26 May 2018).

NASUWT Northern Ireland (nd) Tackling Pupil Indiscipline. [online] Available at: www.nasuwt.org.uk/uploads/assets/uploaded/ad8eac6a-a3c1-4d8e-a8395db584ae3323.pdf (last accessed 24 May 2018).

National Institue of Mental Health (NIMH) (2018) Major Depression. [online] Available at: www.nimh.nih.gov/health/statistics/major-depression.shtml (last accessed 25 May 2018).

Ofsted (2013) The Report of Her Majesty's Chief Inspector of Education, Children's Services and Skills. [online] Available at: www.gov.uk/government/publications/ofsted-annual-report-201213-schools-report (last accessed 24 May 2018).

Ofsted (2014) Below the Radar: Low-level Disruption in the Country's Classrooms. [online] Available at: https://assets.publishing.service.gov.uk/government/uploads/system/uploads/attachment_data/file/379249/Below_20the_20radar_20-_20low-level_20disruption_20in_20the_20country_E2_80_99s_20classrooms.pdf (last accessed 24 May 2018).

Ofsted (2015) Common Inspection Framework: Education, Skills and Early Years from September 2015. [online] Available at: www.gov.uk/government/publications/common-inspection-framework-education-skills-and-early-years-from-september-2015 (last accessed 24 May 2018).

Organisation for Economic Co-operation and Development (OECD) (2010) *PISA 2009 Results: What Makes a School Successful? Resources, Polices and Practices*, Vol IV. Paris: OECD Publishing. [online] Available at: www.oecd.org/pisa/pisaproducts/48852721.pdf (last accessed 6 May 2014).

Pickhardt, C E (2013) *Surviving Your Child's Adolescence: How to Understand and Even Enjoy the Rocky Road to Independence*. San Francisco, CA: Jossey-Bass.

TALIS (2013) Teaching and Learning International Survey: Main Findings from the Survey and Implications for Education andTraining Policies in Europe. [online] Available at: http://ec.europa.eu/dgs/education_culture/repository/education/library/reports/2014/talis_en.pdf (last accessed 3 July 2018).

Vigdor, J L and Ladd, H F (2010) *Scaling the Digital Divide: Home Computer Technology and Student Achievement*. NBER Working Paper No. 16078. [online] Available at: www.nber.org/papers/w16078 (last accessed 26 May 2018).

2 Young people and behaviour

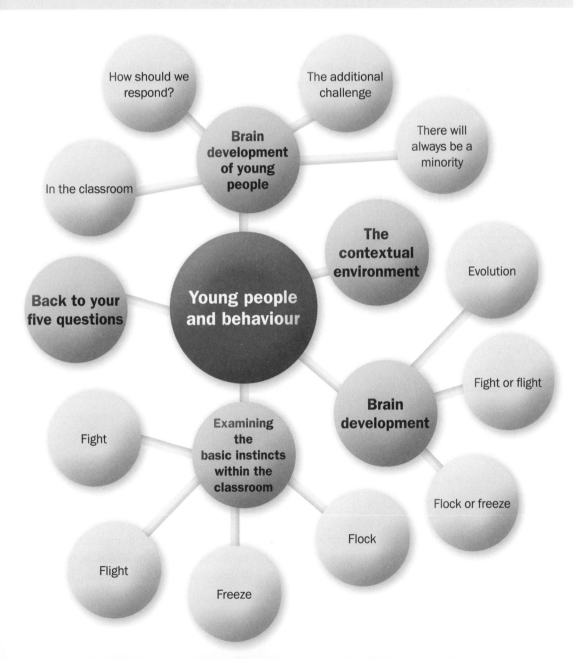

An understanding heart is everything in a teacher, and cannot be esteemed highly enough. One looks back with appreciation to the brilliant teachers, but with gratitude to those who touched our human feeling. The curriculum is so much necessary raw material, but warmth is the vital element for the growing plant and for the soul of the child.

Carl Jung, Swiss psychologist (1875–1961)

Introduction

Throughout your teaching career, you will witness various types of physical and emotional behaviour in your classroom and around the school. You will almost certainly experience dramatic outbursts of anger and callous forms of selfishness, just as you will experience care, kindness and empathy.

It will be necessary to understand the behaviour you are observing, but also to carefully consider your reaction in response to what you are seeing.

Whenever I talk to colleagues about behaviour, I always refer to two areas of understanding. The first relates to the contextual environment in which our young people are growing up (as referred to in Chapter 1). The second area of understanding is that of our students' brain development and related emotional and personality traits.

The contextual environment

Throughout your career you will need to look for ways to manage, get through to, or simply understand the motives and attitude of particular students. I often wish there was a simple answer: I would write it up and send you off armed with the skills to tackle whatever comes your way. What I can provide, however, is some understanding of what you need to ask about the student in order to find the right approach to the situation. All too often, teachers will ask only a few questions and then proceed to tackle the issue in the same old way, without any regard for the particular student or context of the issue. A more open approach is needed, and I would like you to start by examining your initial approach to a particular issue.

Critical question

Imagine that a teacher comes to you for advice: 'What should I do? Billy became really angry and was unacceptably rude to me when I asked him to move to sit in another seat. Then he stormed out of the room.'

» *Jot down five questions you might ask in order to make some rational sense of this situation and establish strategies to support the teacher in avoiding it becoming a recurring issue.*

Obviously, an immediate consideration would be in relation to any special needs that have been identified for Billy, as these would be integral to your thought processes in terms of information needed to support appropriate actions and responses. For this exercise, Billy has no diagnosed special needs.

At the end of this chapter, I will be asking you to reflect back to your five questions, and to consider, in the light of further thinking, whether you would wish to reconsider the information you would require in order to offer support for this member of staff.

As mentioned, there are a number of issues that you need to consider, and I will outline these below.

Brain development

In understanding the influence of brain development and emotional and personality traits on behaviour, I think it important to firstly consider aspects of our evolution as a human species.

Evolution

Some 180 years ago, palaeontologists unearthed the first human fossil attributed to Homo sapiens. After decades of debate, paleoanthropologists now agree that the genetic and fossil evidence suggests that the modern human species – Homo sapiens – evolved in Africa between 100,000 and 200,000 years ago. If we think back to the period between 175 000 BC and 35 000 BC, we are focusing on 140,000 years. Using 45 years as an average 'generation', we can think of this in terms of over 3111 generations. Throughout this lengthy period of time, human development was reasonably slow, as our predecessors hunted and gathered to address their daily needs. Although human demands at this time may be viewed as basic, there was the absolute need for the brain to function on instinct – reacting to emotions, reacting to possible threats.

The last 2,000 years have seen a steady growth of cultures, scientific discoveries and the foundation of renowned places of learning, such as schools and universities, to teach us and to prepare us for the world. This has taken place over a period of some 44 generations.

The age of rapid invention and change in which we now live has brought with it an outstanding growth in technology: the first artificial satellite, Sputnik, came into existence in 1957. Since then, advances have been phenomenal. Just imagine how the human brain must have needed to develop over this period of just two generations.

Two pairs of these basic instincts – fight or flight and flock or freeze – are particularly relevant to our understanding of behaviour in the classroom, behaviour that has its foundations in those 3111 generations learning how to deal with stressful or life-threatening situations.

Fight or flight

We are introduced to the hard-wired basic response of fight or flight at an early age as we seek to make sense of the world and respond to events that raise our anxiety or that are seen as a possible threat. These responses can be measured by the chemical reactions in our brain, which activate different parts of our body to be ready to fight for survival or run for survival. The reality of fight or flight was very real for our ancestors, but it is not always the measured response in the less dangerous environment in which we find ourselves today. We may want to run away from the tax bill or final demand, or we may want to hit someone who is shouting at us, but very rarely, thankfully, are those events matters of life and death.

Similarly, the stresses that occur within a classroom are not a matter of life and death. However, the body will still respond as it is hard-wired to do if the classroom environment or the teacher causes stress or anxiety. Therefore, although it is difficult for someone who isn't anxious to understand the seemingly dramatic reactions of another, it is important to remember they are acting in an entirely human way, and that this needs to be handled with respect and consideration.

Flock or freeze

The flock or freeze instinct is also a natural response to times of stress and anxiety. The desire to 'flock' stems from a need to be with people with whom we feel safe, to find others in the same situation and get comfort from them. This partly explains why young people can often be found in groups or gangs.

To 'freeze' is to shut down our mind and body and hope that the situation will go away. This is why banks have to repeatedly request those who are getting into debt to talk to them as they find that people in bad situations start to switch off communication and stop opening letters.

Critical questions

» *What do you think is your natural response to stress?*

» *How can you manage your stress levels to keep them relevant to the reality of the situation?*

» *How can you control your instincts to fight (argue), flight (storm off), flock (form a group of like-minded disgruntled people) or freeze (ignore what needs to be confronted and hope it goes away)?*

Examining the basic instincts within the classroom

The classroom environment is, by its very nature, a stressful place for some. It is natural, therefore, to see some of the age-old responses to stress manifesting themselves. This is why it is very important to respond to student stress with methods of reducing and managing it, rather than simply punishing 'bad' behaviour.

Fight

The 'fight' instinct can manifest itself through shouting, name calling, swearing and throwing things, sometimes at people. This will usually be accompanied by the student pacing about and not wanting others to be too close to them. Their body language will become attenuated, demonstrating their annoyance and frustration. I once witnessed a situation in which a teacher became so frustrated with a student for walking too slowly into the classroom after being told off, thinking it was simply caused by a poor attitude, that he made the student go outside and walk in more quickly. Ultimately, this lack of understanding caused the relationship to break down, and any hope of getting positive work from the student vanished.

Flight

If situations are not resolved by defusing the student's anxiety and allowing them time to move from a heightened emotional state to a calmer one, then they may choose to flee.

This reaction includes walking out of the classroom, refusing to come to lessons or even to school itself. Oddly enough, most students don't go very far and tend to stay in the school grounds, and often they go back to the place where the situation has caused the stressful response. A bit like the criminal returning to the scene of the crime.

Freeze

When choosing to 'freeze', a student often refuses to engage. If a student is in a classroom, has been removed from the classroom or has even taken themselves away, then they may just sit on the floor with their head down, not responding to questions or wanting to engage at all.

This is the sign that the person is experiencing the extremes of stress. Nothing within them can help, they cannot fight or run away, they freeze and do nothing. It is the last defensive act that a human can do when in the presence of an animal they are trying to avoid: lie still, do nothing and hope it goes away. I advise teachers that when a young person is in this stage if they shout and become aggressive and react then that is potentially the first sign of improvement.

Remember that if a student is behaving like this then they will need time to come down from the heightened state before they will be able to speak. Any attempt to talk or be near them may elevate the anxiety and cause them to walk away again. You can see how they cope with you standing close or eventually sitting with them, but a slow approach, gauging how the student is doing, will help give reassurance. Tone of voice at this point needs to be calm and unemotional.

Flock

When following this instinct, students will seek peers to join in with chosen behaviour. Meeting with friends will allow them some calm, and as they hang about together they will probably engage in 'mischief', which is, I believe, a form of group bonding behaviour often carried out at the expense of the situation or the place that is causing them stress. They may graffiti, or cause damage to buildings or break the rules by smoking or climbing out of windows. They are doing this to help them take control of the situation or place that is causing them stress.

With all the above, might our students be selecting a particular response because their brain is telling them they are about to encounter a situation with which they feel unable to cope?

What we need to remember at this point is that the body and brain are hard-wired to respond in particular ways to stressful situations. We need to be aware that not only are students triggered by events but so are we – if we are going to manage a stressful situation successfully it is vital that we keep calm.

Critical questions

»   *What physical signs have you noticed within yourself when dealing with disturbance?*

»   *What physical stance do you adopt when dealing with poor behaviour and how much is this influenced by what you are feeling or how you have chosen to stand?*

»   *Where can you place the category of response from students in relation to their stress when you have had to intervene?*

Brain development of young people

It is important to link this understanding of our body's instinctive response to fear and stress with our learning in relation to the brain development of our young people. You can more fully appreciate that development does occur by asking yourself what your earliest memory is. The answer will likely relate to when you were about the age of two-and-a-half or three. This is because, by then, the part of the brain which stores long-term memory had developed enough to be in operation.

Just as science, electronics and communication have advanced rapidly over the last 25 years, so has the ability to study the workings and development of the human brain.

The previous assumption was that the volume of grey matter was highest in very early child-hood, and gradually fell from this point in time. However, more recent findings shift the time-line of brain maturation into adolescence and young adulthood. Researchers at the National Institute of Mental Health (NIMH) and the University of Los Angeles (UCLA) have determined that high-order brain centres, such as the prefrontal cortex, only fully develop when an individual reaches their mid-twenties, due to late changes in the volume of grey matter that forms the thin folding outer layer, or cortex, of the brain (NIMH, 2004). The cortex is where the processes of thought and memory are based; it is often referred to as the CEO of the brain as it is the place that takes control of the rest. When talking to students, I often refer to the two parts of the brain that control how they manage themselves: they can either use the thinking part of the brain or the emotional part of the brain. Unfortunately, the emotional part of the brain is far more easily triggered.

The research also suggests that parts of the cortex mature at different rates. Areas involved in more basic functions mature first – for example, those involved in the processing of sensory information and in movement control. The parts of the brain responsible for more top-down control, such as controlling impulses and planning ahead, the hallmarks of adult behaviour, are almost the last to mature (NIMH 2011).

Put quite simply, over the time that the student is with you, their brain will be undergoing developmental changes of maturity in which they will start not only to be able to access different areas to help them control their emotional behaviour but also to learn how to handle situations. They will be developing methods that will stay with them in later life. It is therefore important that we try to coach and guide them as they master techniques for understanding and controlling their behaviour as they go through these stages.

CASE STUDY

Teaching teenagers about the brain

I once offered to take a Year 9 class who were being disruptive within lessons to teach them about what is going on in their brains and how they can start to develop more control. I had ready a presentation linking the evolution of humans, including discussions about the skills needed to cope with the world thousands of years ago and the need for the brain to handle stressful challenging situations. I was prepared for the group, but when I arrived I was given nine Year 7 lads who had demonstrated that they could not cope well in class and were proving to be very disruptive. The head teacher said, 'We thought you could start with them instead.'

I formed a circle around me and spent time quickly getting to know them and forming a relationship, and they were chatting quite happily with me when one asked what we were going to do. I told him we were going to look at how the brain has developed and what is going on with our own brains.

Because of the way that they were coping with not only me but the school as well, I knew already that the process on which I was wanting to build was out of their range as a group and would have been better suited to a one-on-one session.

One student then wanted to tell me something and kept saying, 'Victor, Victor, Victor, can I tell you this please?' I decided to use this person's emotional excitement to demonstrate to the group how he would be unable to follow a basic command because of the overriding desire of the emotional part of his brain. The others looked on as I said to this lad that I would listen to him but he needed first to let me speak for 30 seconds. His response was, 'Yes, I will, but first I have to tell you this'! I turned to the rest and highlighted, 'See, his brain hasn't yet learnt the method of controlling the strong motivating desire of his emotions.'

At this point, the others started to get bored and asked how long this was going to go on for. I responded by telling them that it was because their brains hadn't yet reached the point where they could deal with this kind of conversation. So I changed the lesson to meet their needs.

It took longer than a week to help them understand the information I was trying to give them.

The point is that we have to recognise we are dealing with individuals whose brain development needs to be taken into account when we are asking them to do things. Up until the age of 15, it's far harder to get a person to manage their emotions once they have become triggered. From the age of 15, it gets easier to coach an individual to take more responsibility for their actions. Like most things in human development, this is only a rough guide, as some will be maturing faster and others may have other issues that are contributing to the situation. What it is important to realise is that talking to Years 1 through to 3 and then years 4 through 6 will be different as they start to view themselves differently, learn about friendships and social clues. Then they start to look for independence and play at being more 'grown up'. Working with Years 7, 8, 9, 10 and 11 is going to be different because their brains are processing the information differently. A conversation like the one I had with those Year 7s was very different from the one I had with the Year 9s. I therefore did not get annoyed with the impatience and poor behaviour of the Year 7 boys but dealt with it and helped them learn appropriate responses.

You may be wondering what you can do with a student in a Year 7 class like the one I had who wanted to tell me something. Well, to start with, nothing. On the first occasion it happens, listen to them and let him or her have the one or two sentences, but don't engage in a conversation, as they are interrupting and should not be allowed to hijack your train of thought. As soon as appropriate, you will have to have a one-to-one chat with them and talk through things that they can do when it happens the next time and teach them what is appropriate. You are training and coaching good behaviour; punishing poor behaviour tends to build resentment and frustration on both sides.

In the classroom

As a teacher, it is important that you appreciate the unfairness of expecting teenagers to have adult levels of organisational skills and decision-making, if their brains are still progressing through phases of development.

Adolescence has been described as having four stages. One of these is disorganisation; the others being having a bad attitude, rebellion and early experimenting. Young people want to take more control of their lives yet haven't learned the skills necessary to do so. We can help them to find strategies and ways to manage, which is a much better approach than setting sanctions for them when they mis-manage.

The delayed development of the prefrontal cortex means many teenagers are simply not equipped to recognise the full consequences of their actions. This is the reason for the continued debate as to the age when children can be held accountable for their actions within the criminal court. During these adolescent years, children are still trying to understand society and deal with their own inner battles of peer pressure, lack of direction, impulsiveness and lack of identity. It is therefore considered by some to be unjust to convict them in the same manner as adults.

The part of a teenage brain responsible for emotional responses is fully active, though, maybe even more so than an adult's. However, the ability to keep emotional and impulsive responses in check is yet to reach maturity. This imbalance does provide some clues as to the teenage tendency to act on impulse, without regard to risk. A 35-year-old brain will appreciate that joyriding isn't a great choice of activity but, for the thrill-seeking, emotionally charged, exploring teenager this may not be the case. Throwing a piece of paper during a chemistry lesson may be interpreted by an adult as an extremely risky thing to do, but when measured against what a teenager may be experiencing, it is way down on their level of risk.

Teenagers are developing more abstract thought and critical-thinking skills. This may instigate a questioning of rules and the testing of boundaries, often resulting in discord at home as well as in the classroom. You may encounter complaints about perceived inconsistencies – *'Why am I being told off and not Hannah?'*, *'Mr Smith lets us in his class, why don't you?'*

Behaviour challenges at this developmental stage have long been accepted and present nothing new to us. G Stanley Hall wrote *'the ages from 14 to 24 are the years when unruly behaviours of all kinds are at their peak'* (cited in Arnett, 2006). Your students are being presented with a great deal of complex contradictory information, and they are trying hard to make sense of it all.

Critical questions

» *When do you praise your students for acting in a caring and considerate manner?*

» *At what point in your lesson can you make sure that students are not being controlled by their natural responses to stress?*

» *How often do you look to see what the stress trigger was rather than just dealing with the consequences?*

How should we respond?

As educators, it is important to acknowledge that, in terms of sheer intellectual power, an adolescent brain is a match for an adult's. The capacity of a person to learn will never be greater than during adolescence (NIMH, 2011).

Although an adolescent brain hasn't fully developed, that doesn't mean it's not fit for purpose. It just means that teenagers need support and guidance in learning how to control and manage themselves in a way that avoids behaviour that is destructive to themselves and others. Puberty and into early adult years is a particularly critical time for brain sculpting to take place.

I recall a conversation with a student who was explaining to me that there was no need for him to get out of bed early every day to come into school, because he had secured a place at college and he was predicted to get the exam grades he needed. I responded to this by saying I could almost guarantee that, if he continued to attend school only on an ad hoc basis, he would struggle to be successful at college. When the calendar moves to the start of the college year, he wouldn't suddenly be wide awake in the morning, because his brain was currently being trained to still be asleep at that time.

Consistency in expectations for teenagers is vital, along with allowing them to at least feel they have played a role in establishing the perimeters of acceptable behaviour. Teens crave information and opinions, but don't want to be told what to do. They have a great sense of their own need to be in control. The best approach, therefore, is to permit age-appropriate decision-making. Explain, with reasons they will understand, why there is sometimes no choice to be made. Help them understand rules as a component of a sharing society.

In supporting teenagers to understand the importance of emotional control, I have found it helpful to explain my understanding of brain development and the impact this has on responses to situations. In supporting teachers, I am always clear about the importance of not taking inappropriate student comments personally and ensuring absolute control of their own feelings and reactions.

The additional challenge

Adolescence is also the stage of development when young people become very susceptible to the influences of peers (Tate, 2006). How they appear and act in front of other teenagers is often more important than their relationship with you as a teacher. It is absolutely vital, therefore, to secure influence through respect, care and support, rather than an authoritarian approach. There is a need to guide our teenagers to analyse and process the world around them, manage negative peer pressure and gain problem-solving skills to manage life's challenges. You are equipping teenagers for life, as well as providing them with an education.

There are other factors to consider during this period of adolescence that will impact upon the classroom and learning. Mackinlay, Charman and Kermiloff-Smith (2003) studied the development of prospective memory. (This is the memory that includes simple tasks of everyday life – examples include: remembering to put clothes in the laundry basket; turning off lights when leaving a room; remembering to bring in your homework – all things that we expect young people and students to do all the time.) A multi-task paradigm was used to test children aged between 6 and 14 and adults. Participants were scored for both efficiency and the strategies used to carry out the tasks effectively. A significant improvement in both efficiency and quality of strategies was found between the ages of 6 and 10. However, between the ages of 10 and 14 there was no significant change in performance – at the time when they change schools and are expected to meet the organisational demands of a secondary school. We as educators need to appreciate we have to help them develop those strategies during this time.

There will always be a minority

The vast majority of your students will recognise the importance of their conformity in society, and that includes in your classroom. However, there will always be teenagers who have not yet reached the necessary level of maturity or have learnt ways to use inappropriate behaviour to avoid aspects of life they find stressful or difficult and haven't found the necessary skills to overcome those issues.

These young people may well have already found themselves falling behind in their learning. Continual disruption, and maybe persistent absence from lessons, will almost certainly lead to feelings of detachment from the learning process. There will also tend to be a flocking together of common allies who have adopted the same behaviour. It is your role, as the adult, to take steps to build a positive relationship with this minority group, ensuring an atmosphere of inclusion that avoids isolation within your classroom.

Back to your five questions

The exercise at the beginning of this chapter involved you deciding on five questions to ask a colleague, in order to support him/her appropriately in addressing a classroom behaviour challenge.

It may be that you now wish to reconsider the information you would require about the student. In light of what you have read in this chapter, would you still ask the same questions?

My own personal thoughts would be the need to ascertain the following information:

1.   **What age is the student?**

    This will certainly have some influence on his thought processes when being asked to move seats. Classroom instructions may well be interpreted differently and your own emotional intelligence is important in being able to combat possible inbuilt, automatic inappropriate responses.

    An 11/12-year-old student may well try to push boundaries, due to frustration in having to conform to classroom expectations. They are far more used to being influenced by the emotional part of the brain and this will cause them to make quick emotional responses to situations rather than measured considered ones.

    A 14/15-year-old is perhaps attempting to ensure they are 'in charge', and the instruction to move seats is a challenge to them as well as showing them up in front of their peers, which brings about the fight or flight mode of response.

    Once a student has reached 16/17 and they are beginning to establish their own place in the world, they may perceive moving seats as an opportunity to challenge your decision and provide an alternative in light of their perceived measured understanding.

2.   **How do you, yourself, feel about the incident?**

    It is important to find out if the colleague is also being influenced by the automatic responses to stress. He/she has asked for help, but is this just to check if it's all right to feel annoyed and to find a colleague with whom to share his/her feelings?

    With this question, you are also ascertaining how your colleague initially responded to the situation. Did they, through their attitude and tone, escalate or de-escalate the outburst?

Question 3 assumes the teacher reacted calmly and in a way that would normally de-escalate a challenging situation.

3.   **Do you know of anything else that is going on in the student's life at the moment?**

    Did influences outside your colleague's classroom contribute to this particular outburst? Consider the well-known opening of the fizzy-drink bottle demonstration, when the first person to whom the bottle is handed opens it immediately. After being slightly shaken, it is given to a second person, who is more careful as they unscrew the top. A third person receives the bottle after far more vigorous shaking, and they very slowly and cautiously deal with their challenge to open the bottle.

    If an unsuspecting person is given the bottle to open at this stage, unaware of the vigorous shaking, they will be initially surprised at the result as the bottle is opened, but they will also realise, quite quickly, that it was the result of someone else's actions that caused the inevitable eruption.

Likewise, the teacher is often the innocent recipient of a response that was aggravated by other sources, with the reaction to the instruction being a vent for already established feelings.

4.   Does the student react in a similar way in other lessons?

This will elicit information as to the extent of the student's ability to manage his/ her emotions and whether support is required in addressing more deep-seated frustrations. As well as being a subject teacher, your colleague is also a guide and mentor in terms of the student's wider development and well-being.

If this type of behaviour only manifests itself in your colleague's lessons, why is this the case? Can successful approaches and strategies adopted elsewhere be identified and established in this particular subject area?

5.   What are your plans for meeting with the student?

This final question is absolutely vital and relates to how the teacher wants things to move forward. For the incident not to happen again, the relationship between student and teacher will have to be addressed before any learning can be re-established.

Many teachers, understandably, find the prospect of such a meeting very difficult. Some will actually completely avoid any follow-up discussion. However, your colleague is the adult and, therefore, has to take the lead in demonstrating how to respond positively to a range of situations that will emerge throughout the young person's life. Simply hoping that the next lesson will be different is asking for trouble.

I am absolutely sure that asking your colleague these five questions will help establish an understanding that the behaviour challenge he/she experienced was not necessarily the student's fault and neither was it a failing on the part of him/her as a teacher.

In order to ascertain the reasons for students' behaviour in our classrooms, there is an absolute need to consider a much wider picture.

CASE STUDY

I was engaged in doing a learning walk with a deputy head of a secondary school and we noticed a boy from Year 7 was outside the lesson looking back into the class and pulling faces at the other students. As we walked closer he stopped and stood there whilst he was asked what he was doing. We had the very typical comments about the reason why he had been sent out of class and I was informed that it was unfortunately becoming fairly typical for him to be seen outside of lessons.

When the teacher came out from his lesson I took the opportunity to ask to see the boy's work. As the child had been in the school for five months from the start in September I was interested in seeing his progress to date. Looking back through his work we could see a gradual decline in class work, a rise in doodles and some very good colouring-in. I asked him about his understanding and of the subject and we all could see how it had not kept pace with the learning of others and this pattern had in fact been easy to track with the rise in his alternative behaviour within class.

As a school they undertook a round robin of all his class subjects to check on his progress and understanding throughout. It was a simple process to look, identify and react to what the student had been showing through his work and what was the possible cause of his behaviour. Marking of books should also be an indication of someone's emotional state relating to the lesson as well as their educational one.

Chapter reflections

» *The aim of this chapter was to look at the influences of evolutionary and physical development on behaviour.*

» *With this knowledge, we are better able to evaluate what we are seeing and hearing and therefore provide a far more measured response to situations we will face on a daily basis in our classrooms and around the school.*

» *We have looked at how, as humans, we are conditioned to react in a certain way to moments of stress or anxiety. We have also seen that there are a number of questions we can ask our students to provide a good indication as to the cause of anxiety that manifests itself in lessons.*

» *This understanding is vital in allowing us to support our students who are exhibiting signs of stress in our classrooms and to manage behaviour effectively. As educators, we are given the task of developing students' academic ability at a time when they are experiencing the major transition from childhood to adulthood.*

» *Physical changes, alongside brain growth and development, are taking place throughout all stages of secondary school life. Our students, therefore, need a huge amount of guidance, support and understanding. Arguments and frustrations are all part of the changes that take place as they find their own place in the world and the society in which they belong.*

Next steps

The next stage of our understanding in becoming effective educators has to be in relation to considering ourselves. What have been our influences? What drives us to be the excellent teachers that we wish to be?

Your involvement is critical for some of the most vulnerable students as they need to learn to problem solve and interact correctly with others. I believe that students who struggle within class are not only stressed with the feeling of inadequacy academically, they often also feel inadequate in being able to explain their difficulty as well and solve the problem they face.

This causes them to become confrontational with others or simply difficult to settle within the class. Think about how you can help students within your class develop the skills to discuss ways to overcome problems or issues and to examine consequences of actions. Young people like to look for acceptance from others, they like to feel in control and they also like to be recognised for who they are. Look for ways that you can help those who are more isolated within the class gain those things by working collaboratively with others. Influences outside of the classroom may have impacted their lives greatly and affected all three of the foundations they are looking for, so make your classroom a place where they can find them.

Taking it further

In order to gain further insight into the probable experiences of our young people during perceived stressful periods of time, it is worth considering the body's automatic physiological responses to a situation we may ourselves view as threatening. A very good process to go through to understand this can be found at www.healthcentral.com/ency/408/guides/000031_2.html.

See also http://reclaimingjournal.com/sites/default/files/journal-article-pdfs/09_4_Tate.pdf.

References

Arnett, J J (2006) G Stanley Hall's *Adolescence*: Brilliance and Nonsense. *History of Psychology* 9(3), 186–97.

Mackinlay, R, Charman, T and Kermiloff-Smith, A (2003) *Remembering to Remember: A Developmental Study of Prospective Memory in a Multitasking Paradigm*. Biennial Meeting of the Society for Research in Child Development, Tampa, FL.

NIMH (2004) *Imaging Study Shows Brain Maturing*. [online] Available at: www.sciencedaily.com/releases/2004/05/040518074211.htm (last accessed 26 May 2018).

NIMH (2011) *The Teen Brain: Still Under Construction*. [online] Available at: https://infocenter.nimh.nih.gov/pubstatic/NIH%2011-4929/NIH%2011-4929.pdf (last accessed 26 May 2018).

Tate, T F (2006) Peer Influences and Positive Cognitive Restructuring. *Cyc-Online, Reading for Child and Youth Care People*, 84. The International Child and Youth Care Network.

3 Understanding self

Knowing yourself is the beginning of all wisdom.

Aristotle

Introduction

Over the past two chapters, I have discussed ways to increase your understanding of the changing social environment in which students are growing up and how you can learn more about their physical and emotional changes and development. The quotation from Carl Jung at the beginning of the previous chapter helps in appreciating the importance of the caring nature that teachers need in order to bring out the best in our students. This further quotation from Jung (1923) moves us neatly into the next part of the book:

> *Your vision will become clear only when you can look into your own heart. Who looks outside, dreams; who looks inside, awakens.*

During this chapter I want you to take some time to reflect upon those people who have influenced you, what they said or did that had such an impact. I also want you to think about what caused you to choose the career path of teaching. It is when we appreciate what motivates us and directs our thoughts and desires that we start to understand how and why we react to things.

Teachers need to stay calm and composed in the classroom; as well as being inspirational and excellent leaders we are going to be role models for them in so many different areas of their lives. It is important to remain consistent in our approach to this, in order to not become diverted from the path along which we are walking, letting students see that we have a plan and vision that includes them.

It will therefore help a great deal to spend time reflecting more about yourself so that when the going gets tough you have a clear picture of the foundation on which you are building, and a chance to remind yourself what is truly important to you.

Reflection

Whenever I talk with a teacher who is going through a tough time at school, I ask them these questions.

* Why did you get into teaching?
* What was it that made the choice for you?

These questions help them look back to the start of their career and try to capture the force that motivated them.

To start this time of reflection for yourself, I want you to consider your answers to the following questions. Record the answers, with the date on which you answered them, as a record of how your thoughts or ideas change or don't change over your teaching career.

Why have you chosen teaching as a career? The following are some possible responses, but it is important to find the answer that is truly yours.

*   I was inspired by a teacher and wanted to do the same.

*   I have a passion for the subject and want to share it.

*   I love passing on knowledge.

*   It has always been my chosen career (even played at being a teacher with teddies).

*   I wanted to change careers and teaching looked good.

*   Nothing else looked any good.

*   I love working with young people.

*   I followed what my parents did.

*   I wanted to give something to society.

*   I felt called by God.

What is the best thing about the job?

*   The people I work with.

*   The students.

*   The freedom in your classroom.

*   Your form group.

*   The holidays.

*   The chance of promotion.

*   The money.

*   Feeling a part of a team.

*   Inspiring others about a subject.

You will be surprised at the variety of answers I get in response to these questions. This is just a small sample, but it is a very good motivational tool, as it helps understand why people continue to thrive in what can be a very stressful situation.

What is your own personal vision or philosophy of life?

Helen Keller, one of the most well-known blind people who has ever lived, was once asked what would be worse than being born blind. Her answer: *'To have sight without vision.'*

It is important to think through what you are aiming to achieve on a variety of fronts that meet your personal goal and philosophy of life. This should include your family, your work and your career as well as your personal life. It needs to be the very mantra that drives you and moves throughout all that you are seeking to accomplish. Try to be as brief as you can and also try to make sure that it is one that can be easily explained to others.

I like two words, *excellence* and *fun*. Consider this:

> If you don't do it excellently, don't do it at all, because if it's not excellent, it won't be profitable or fun, and if you're not in the business for fun or for profit, what the hell are you doing there?
>
> (Townsend, 2007, p 40)

Throughout my family, work and personal life, I try to keep those two words in mind. They enable me to question what I am doing and to check I am achieving my standards of excellence and fun. I expect those working for me to know that this is a philosophy that also includes them. It enables me to direct conversations using those words as a marker of my standard to work towards. Notice I use *my* standards, as this is personal philosophy: I could ask lots of people what they understand to be the meaning of those words and they will also respond with a slightly different slant.

Critical questions

»   *Who has had the most influence on your life to date?*

»   *Have they taught you things that now direct your life in a positive manner?*

»   *Are you influenced more by your culture than your own personal beliefs?*

»   *How much of 'you' do you bring to the classroom to motivate others towards their own greatness?*

The importance of a good foundation

Creating a foundation for yourself is as important as having a firm foundation for a house. Spending time learning about your motivations helps you to become more unshakeable when the hardships of life come and pay a visit. The main thing to bear in mind is that it is your life; fulfil what is true to you, otherwise you will spend far too long trying to look for the approval of others. As it says in the poem 'The Guy in the Glass':

> For it isn't your mother, your father or wife whose judgment upon you must pass, but the man whose verdict counts most in your life is the one staring back from the glass.
>
> (Wimbrow, 1934)

Once you have your conclusion as to why you have chosen teaching, and your motivating factor for becoming an excellent teacher, remember they are the factors driving you forward towards the goal you set yourself, your own vision.

Setting yourself a philosophy and vision is important both for yourself and for your class and the individuals within your class. People are motivated by those with a passion and a vision for what is possible. One of the many debilitating factors within classrooms today is the lack of passion and enthusiasm towards learning; students don't see that what they are doing will in fact help them later in life. No amount of telling them will help them to say '*You know what, you are right. I will try harder*'. If they don't believe in themselves and what is possible for them then this belief, passion and enthusiasm has to come from you. You may well be the most positively influential part of their lives, and unless you can see beyond what you are looking at and dealing with, and inspire others to be able to do the same, then you will have difficulty getting the best out of some of your more challenging students and will never move from the ordinary into the excellent.

Are you inspiring?

I spoke to a group of teachers about emotionally intelligent leadership, looking at the differences between leadership and management. They recognised that leadership involves setting a vision and inspiring people to work towards it, whereas management involves ensuring systems, policies and people are working together. With this basic idea of the differences in mind, I then asked, what words do we use at the start of the year or with a new group that are visionary and inspiring, and enable us to be both leaders and managers within a classroom?

When you have to introduce yourself to a new group of students, take time to think about the following.

How inspiring are your words? Are they about processes and work that needs to be done, exams that will be passed or taken, the structure of the lessons and rules for the classroom? That's *management*.

Or are they about the journey you are going to be taking them on personally as they grow physically, mentally and socially? How you are going to help them get excited about the possibilities of the subject and what doors it will open for them through their lives? How you will get to know them and enjoy seeing how they achieve and work together towards making the class into one of the best experiences within school? That's *inspiring leadership*.

The first words that you say, the philosophy and vision that you share, will be the foundation on which the rest of the learning is built. Keep revisiting it throughout the year, keep reminding students they are on a journey with you and you are keen and excited to be their teacher.

Critical questions

» *What words sum up your vision for yourself?*

» *What words sum up your vision for your classroom?*

» *What words sum up your philosophy towards those you meet?*

» *Do you see the classroom as a place of work or a place to inspire others through your work?*

Understanding reactions

Knowing and being clear about your passions and philosophies of life will also help you understand why certain things annoy you more than others. Have you ever been surprised at the harshness or depth of someone's reaction towards something when to you it was only a minor event? Your own reaction may be even stronger towards a different event. This is often because the event that triggered such a reaction is close to what is most important to you. Why do some people feel more passionate about recycling and saving the planet, while others are more passionate about saving the whales or dolphins, yet others may send money to starving children in Africa, while others are concerned about those with terminal illness, or even testing on animals? We know that the list is endless, but what annoys us in a class-room, what people say, how people react towards one another, how they treat the classroom and the books, how students treat each other, those younger, the support staff, a child with special needs, all of these may prompt a stronger or lesser reaction from others and it is good for you to think through what situations you tackle straight away and those you think are less important and perhaps treat more casually. As students will also pick up on these factors, it is good to be consistent. In addition, what might be less important to you might be very important to another teacher, so you need to give as consistent a response as you can to help the students understand what is expected.

Also, if you do know that something really annoys you, when an incident occurs, try to stay as measured as you can, because if the students see you overreact it will deflect their attention from the actual message of correction you are aiming to give. I have often heard students talk about how 'loopy' a teacher went about something; the 'something' gets demoted in favour of talking about the reaction. Know yourself and be mindful of how you need to get the message across, even when you want to shout it. Shouting at someone doesn't make the message clearer – it blurs it in a fog of emotions. I am aware that on some occasions anger is a healthy emotion to show but, in the words of Aristotle:

> Anyone can become angry – that is easy, but to be angry with the right person and to the right degree and at the right time and for the right purpose and in the right way – that is not within everyone's power and it is not easy.

Critical questions

» How often do you choose to raise your voice, or do you let your emotions choose?

» Has a message ever become clearer to you because someone shouted it?

» What message do you want to get across when you shout, the issue at hand or just your emotions?

Psychometric profiling

Getting to know yourself this intimately is extremely useful. Companies and, more recently, schools are using psychometric profiling to help people understand different members of teams to improve how they work together. They do this by asking questions and, through the answers, obtaining a result which gives a broad outline of personality. The two main types of profiling that I use when working with leaders or aspiring leaders are Belbin®, which looks at the make up of teams, and the Myers–Briggs Type Indicator (MBTI®), which looks at the personality type of an individual.

> *Whatever the circumstances of your life, the understanding of type can make your perception clearer, your judgment sounder, and your life closer to your heart's desire.*

(Briggs Myers, 1995)

We will take a brief look at the MBTI® in more detail to help you develop your understanding about types of personality and how they exhibit themselves within your classroom. This will help you when it comes to dealing with behavioural issues, but also when a student struggles over a specific thing you are trying to teach; the reason they are struggling might not be because the task is hard but because their mind doesn't think in a certain way. It will also help you get a clearer picture of what your preferred working environment (classroom) looks like.

MBTI®

MBTI® aims to make the theory of Carl Jung's psychological types (1923) understandable and useful for those people interested in understanding others better. It aims to show that the supposed random variations in people's behaviour are in fact quite orderly and consistent. It illuminates how people make themselves aware of things, how they interpret others' actions, how they process information and how they come to conclusions. It can be assumed that if a person differs from another in interpretation then they also will differ in their interests, values and perhaps even their skills. Building on this interpretation and the basic preferences implicated in Jung's theory, Isabel Briggs Myers and her mother Katharine Briggs developed the MBTI®, which has established itself worldwide as a valid and reliable instrument through the many hundreds of studies that have been carried out on it since its first publication in 1962. The reason it is a useful tool within school is that it doesn't measure traits, ability or character but does highlight the differences between people, and it's that understanding of differences that needs to be taken into account whenever people have to work closely with each other.

These differences start to show themselves at an early age, as does the frustration that arises when we don't understand the motives and actions of others because they don't think as we do. A lot of time in the classroom and around school will include you trying to get students to see things from each other's view, as well as trying to find different ways to explain things so that they understand you. This will often be the result of the different ways students process information, rather than a poor understanding of the words or theory being used. The more you understand this, the more your knowledge of the students will grow.

So, we know that society has an influence, students' upbringing will have an influence, their own physical and emotional development, which for some will have been very traumatic and for others very caring and loving, will have an influence, and this will all be put together around the type of person they are. You cannot pin a person's behaviour on just one thing, like some are apt to do by saying *'it's their age'*, or *'it's their family upbringing'*, or *'he/she is not very bright'*. True understanding comes with taking into account all these factors, as they will have a bearing upon how different people process information, how they like the noise level when they work, how they regard the information they are being given and how they complete their work. Telling someone off when their methods in any of these areas don't fit what is expected or needed is wrong. They need coaching to help them use what they are naturally inclined to do to get the best for them and to manage the times when things come harder to them.

CASE STUDY

I was observing an English lesson in which the teacher wanted the class to use descriptive language to explore what an author meant in a specific passage. For example, the description of mountains and valleys could have been a description of how two travellers were viewing their lives and what their future was going to be. For some in the class, the excellent descriptions and metaphors came easily and could have been written up as examples for all GCSE students across the land, but one poor student couldn't move on from 'No! The author just wanted to put in mountains and valleys, he wasn't thinking anything else except mountains and valleys!' The problem this student was facing had nothing to do with his inability to use metaphors, it was the way that he was being asked to think he was struggling with. He therefore needed a different explanation to free up his ability to do what the teacher was asking for.

The explanation that I gave to the teacher highlighted the type of person the student was, how he was influenced more by facts and specifics rather than looking at the bigger picture and possibilities. These differences are categorised within the MBTI® by the terms Sensing (S), which favours specifics, facts, reality, past and present experiences, whereas Intuition (N) prefers the bigger picture and possibilities, and isn't tied down to how things are or were but looks for new insights. Each has its own merits but both have to be taken into account when dealing with students, especially when what you are asking favours one more than the other.

How do you think and process information?

In a simple test to see how people process information I place an apple on my hand and ask them to describe what they see. What are the thoughts that first come into their head? Below are some of the answers that people have given me over the years.

One set of answers will be:

•   apple;

•   round;

•   red and green;

- crispy;

- has a stalk.

If I ask the people who are giving these answers to think more widely they may say:

- orchard;

- trees;

- one of your five a day.

Yet all these things still have to do with an apple, the starting point. These are example answers from those who think as 'S'.

For others, their first thought may be:

- William Tell;

- Snow White;

followed by:

- Disneyland Paris;

- holidays.

These are examples of answers that 'N' types might give.

I would have had to spend a great deal of time encouraging those in the first group to make the jump that comes naturally to the second group and, similarly, I would have had to help the second group stay on task, as their mind is apt to jump whenever triggered by comments or thoughts.

As you have been reading this you may have been wondering how you think. I want you to explore who you are, so take the Myers–Briggs test (www.myersbriggs.org/my-mbti-personality-type) as this helps you start to look at the different factors and what you may need to take into account, not only when you teach students but when you work with colleagues.

When speaking to the student who was having difficulty within the English lesson, I needed therefore to deal with the facts for him. I talked about the use of a metaphor, *fact*. I stayed away from linking it to the author because that was when it became a problem for him as he didn't know the author, hadn't spoken to him and couldn't imagine what he would be thinking. So we just looked at how we use metaphors when they are helpful, when he had used them in the past and which ones he could use for mountains and valleys and then also how he could write sentences putting that into the context of the book. So read the passage, look at the descriptions in the passage, and then look at when the words being used could have a double meaning.

Was this still a struggle for him? Yes. Still hard to do? Yes, but no longer impossible and a block for him. For the teacher and some in the class it was exciting to imagine how the author was seeing a bigger picture and letting their minds run with that idea. But, as we have seen, that's not the case for others and does not indicate a problem with English. So the next time the teacher runs that lesson, she first asks who finds it easy to imagine the author meaning different things in a passage and who finds it a struggle to think that the author means anything other than what he has written.

Different personalities in the classroom

There are other highlighted differences between people that are going to demonstrate themselves within the classroom, and I want to take a look at two of them, extroversion and introversion, so you can begin to think about the way you can deal with them, as well as seeing if there are traits that you recognise about yourself.

I am going to give some very general points, as above, that highlight the two differences and it is to be understood that this is a basic introduction into understanding the differences, not a final way of characterising yourself. But I am sure that you will notice the behaviours highlighted and we will look at ways to become better leaders and coaches of those for whom we have responsibility by using our own emotional intelligence.

Within the MBTI®, the differences between extrovert and introvert personality types are characterised by those who gain energy from external things (E) and those who like to recharge their batteries internally (I).

Extroversion (E)

Those who are a very dominant E will demonstrate this by their willingness always to talk, always to be keen to give their opinion, and they will find it hard to be quiet even when they don't have anything to say. They may like to tap things to generate a noise, and they may also talk out loud when looking for something. They will find it hard to be quiet within a lesson and having to work in silence could also be a struggle for them. They will often engage in conversations with others and will look for external distractions. When delivering MBTI® workshops to adult participants I point out that the E types have demonstrated to us all that they are happy to work in groups as it gives them a chance to chat, and they can dominate the group even if they don't always have the best ideas or the most constructive solution to a project. Unfortunately, when this happens within a classroom the E types may well be told repeatedly that they need to be quiet, and they may, if this caution doesn't work, be put on report or made to sit on their own. They will almost definitely have been told to stand out of the classroom to learn to be quiet. Yet these methods will not cause them to learn how to control their preferred method of living their life. They may alter their behaviour when in your presence, or when they are aware that they will be disciplined, yet this is not a coaching method that will help them become self-disciplined.

Later in life, those who like to give their opinions will, in meeting situations, dominate proceedings and not give others the opportunity to finish what they are saying before jumping in with their own thoughts. Not a lot of difference from what you see in the classroom, so if you want to help them develop skills to listen as well as share their opinions then you have to start the work in the classroom.

Critical questions

»   *Do you prefer a quiet classroom and feel calmer when students are working quietly with a very low level of noise or do you prefer to have chatter and see and hear the interaction between students?*

»   *Are there aspects of lessons that excite and interest you more and are they to do with your preference of working and thinking?*

CASE STUDY

In a mathematics lesson, a Year 9 boy who was extremely able and bright was sent out of the lesson because he constantly kept answering the questions while the teacher was trying to find out what others thought. Even when asking the students to write their answers on a personal wipe board and hold them up, he found it hard not to shout out the answer as he was writing it down. When first told to be quiet he lowered his voice and only those in his group had the privilege of hearing his answer. He wasn't telling them, he was just answering it out loud first. When told to be quiet again, he apologised and remained quiet for the next two questions, but found it impossible to remain quiet when a discussion started about why one of the students arrived at their answer. He could hold back no longer so proceeded to tell the teacher what he thought they had done and what they should have done. At that point, the teacher had had enough and he was asked to leave the room. He was crestfallen as it was quite obvious that he enjoyed mathematics and was very keen to do more. He just didn't have the skill to stay quiet.

I had observed the teacher earlier in the lesson, when discussing what was going to take place during the lesson, quite happily include him in the open conversation and let him contribute, and his comments and willingness to help others was very apparent. Yet, as we saw later, to then curb this E tendency was too much for him. Remember, we are also noticing his age and that the forward part of his brain, which is the part that will help him regulate his emotions and actions, hasn't matured enough for him to rely upon it totally just yet, but it is something we can work with.

Attitude

This is clearly not a matter for disciplining or simply telling the student to change his natural type. This is a coaching matter and the attitude needs to be one of helping the students understand what we need from them and providing some strategies that they can use. The mathematics teacher and I talked with the student outside of the classroom. I first highlighted to him that I wasn't going to tell him off and that he wasn't in any trouble, to engage the thinking part of his brain and to get him to stay emotionally relaxed.

I said I was just curious about what had gone on in the lesson and wanted to know if anything similar happened in other classes. He said yes and that he usually got told off, and he tried his best to stop but he didn't quite manage it. I asked him what he had tried to do to stop himself speaking out, and he said he had just tried to be quiet but that didn't work for long.

I asked if he would be interested in trying something to help him learn to control his enthusiasm and not get told off. He said he would.

When people say they want to change and try something new, it's not enough to just get them to say yes, as this is an obvious answer to an obvious question. You need to ask more to get to the motivation of such an answer. When I dug deeper, he said that he just wanted to get on in lessons and not have to keep feeling bad and apologising.

I suggested that we look at a method of limiting the time he said things to only those times when he thought what he had to offer to the whole class or to the teacher was of vital importance. This would help him make choices about when to speak. I gave him a maximum of six times per lesson and he would regulate these himself by handing over to the teacher one lollipop stick per comment. We would supply him with the lollipop sticks at the start of every lesson. When they were all used up, he would have to remain silent for the rest of the lesson, unless the teacher specifically asked him to speak. The look of concern on his face told me that he was contemplating how hard this would be for him. We talked about the difficulties that he thought he would have and also what he would do if he actually used up all his sticks quickly. We were asking him to learn to regulate his behaviour in a way that he had never done before, but in a way that didn't make him feel bad about who he is, but helped him understand and manage himself better.

What I tend to find with this method is that students don't use up all the sticks but hold onto the last one as they are never sure what is going to come and whether or not they will have a good thing to contribute, and they really don't want to miss out on the opportunity of impressing.

I have highlighted just one case, but this is repeated over and over in the classroom, as there are always a good number of students who find it hard to regulate their chatter. Sometimes I have worked with a group of them and explained that they have to learn to manage and that they can support one another in doing so. It will be important for you to find methods of managing them, just as it is important for you to recognise that if you have these tendencies yourself then the chances are that your classroom will be slightly louder than others and that you will be more lenient about low-level disturbance because of it.

Critical questions

» *How do you conduct yourself in meetings? Are you chatty or reflective?*

» *Do you take your time to answer? Are you afraid to give your opinion? Or do you give your opinion more readily, processing your thoughts as you are speaking?*

» *Do you prefer the interaction of people over the quietness of contemplation?*

Introversion (I)

In contrast to extrovert personalities, there are students who are extremely reluctant to give their opinion and find it very hard to speak out – introvert personalities. When asked a question they appear to look at you blankly as if you have just asked them to answer the most impossible question ever imposed upon anyone. They are often dismissed as being shy and reserved, and for some this may well be the case, but for others it's just that they prefer to do their thinking and organising internally and keep their thoughts and comments to themselves. It is just as hard for them to speak out as it is for the E student to be quiet, yet, as teachers, it is important for us to encourage everyone to give their opinion and contribute. These students often go under the radar within school as they are so quiet, and this is often to the detriment of them as well as others in the class, because when they are encouraged to contribute, their comments are usually drawn from lengthy consideration.

They will need to build a good relationship with you, and this may take time, but is very worth it, as you will again be involved in helping them develop within the context of the classroom in a way they will be able to carry forward into the rest of their working lives.

The methods you use to encourage them to speak could include priming them before the lesson that you will be asking them to give an opinion. In this way you avoid the period of silence before they say anything. It will also be important that others listen, as the I-type student will stop talking as soon as someone else starts to speak because they won't want to speak over them (especially those who have a strong E tendency).

CASE STUDY

I was once observing a mathematics lesson in which a teacher asked a quiet, I-type student a very simple question. The student looked surprised at the question, and then just stared blankly at the teacher rather than answering. At this point, the E students began to shout out answers, taking over the situation. The teacher then asked the student an easier question, to which the student just replied 'I don't know.' At this point, the teacher became frustrated and accused the student of being deliberately awkward, pretending not to know the answer to such a simple question. When questioned later, the student said he had felt confused by the teacher's questions, because he thought he was trying to trick him with an easy question – this had caught him off-guard as he was never usually asked anything. The teacher explained that he was trying to encourage the student to speak in class by asking him an easy question.

The understanding drawn from the two case studies demonstrates that the behaviour you experience comes from a variety of causes, and the more emotionally aware you are, the more skills you can use to develop and coach them towards their greatest potential.

More often than not I am asked to deal with E types within schools, as they are seen as a disturbance. The I types are often not taken into account and therefore go unnoticed. However, as a teacher, you will get greater insight and a more accurate reflection upon the level of teaching and understanding within the class if you take the time to encourage the I-type student to say something.

There is a very good method to encourage group discussion, including both E and I students, which involves a ball of string. The first person in the discussion starts with the string. The next person to speak then takes the ball of string with the first person still holding the end.

Over time, the web of string grows and gets tangled, highlighting just who is doing all the talking and who is getting overlooked or keeping themselves on the side-lines. If you agree beforehand the minimum and maximum number of times each person can take the string, this will help make sure that discussions are inclusive.

A further idea for helping to develop both E and I students is to assign group table managers, whose responsibility it is to answer questions set by the teacher regarding findings or work they are engaged in. You can introduce the role of the manager any way you wish, but it is good to provide guidance as to what is expected of them and the team they are working with. If you assign the I student the role of table manager, then you are encouraging them to speak, and if the E is table manager then it means they have to listen to everyone in their team.

Critical questions

»   *In light of what you now know about E and I personality types within your classroom, consider how you will manage those who have a tendency to talk and be loud and how you will encourage those who are quiet.*

»   *How can you introduce an understanding and appreciation of personality differences to your students?*

»   *What can you do to cater for the different ways in which these personality types process information?*

»   *How has your own personality type influenced how you react to situations?*

Highlighting the differences in the classroom

There is something to be said for highlighting the differences within the classroom, and it is when we appreciate the differences that we will be able to develop empathy with others.

There will always be new and different things to introduce to your students, no matter what the subject is. These will include different tools, materials, languages, ingredients, chemicals, musical instruments, sports, formulas, dates, books, structures of languages and spellings. So it is a relatively easy task to introduce students to personal differences. When they understand these differences they will have grasped a good understanding of each other as well. I am sure you understand this, and the sooner the students appreciate each other and work together then the better the classroom will work.

Highlighting the differences in working life

With the openness to learn about the differences within the classroom you can also examine your own preferred work style and environment. These will impact on how you teach, communicate and contribute to the school. The main aim is not to wish you were more like someone else but learn to accept and get the best from who you are.

All the above items are there to help you learn more about being an emotionally intelligent leader as you develop your career. The many challenges that you will repeatedly face in the classroom, staff room and life will be better managed if you understand how your actions and emotions are affecting those around you. This can only happen with a good clear under-standing of how self-aware you are, how self-regulated you can become, and knowing how to motivate yourself and others in a positive way, demonstrating empathy and social skills. With these skills in place you will become more successful in all that you aim to do. This is an ongoing task as you develop your emotionally intelligent leadership skills.

Chapter reflections

» *We started the chapter by looking at why you chose teaching as your career, and what your personal vision is for yourself, why you do what you do and who motivated you. We then looked at how are you going to be a motivating factor for others.*

» *Understanding personality types and how people process information in different ways will help you improve your teaching methods and deal with behavioural issues. If you wish to look more closely at the MBTI®, there are many opportunities to access registered facilitators (of which I am one). Registered facilitators will be more than happy to explain in greater detail about the personal implications and the merits of adopting the system within the classroom as well as the workplace.*

» *It is important to ask questions of students and look beyond the first impression into possible causes of behaviour. There may be a myriad of reasons and the only one who has the answer is the person who is standing in front of you. It is vital that you spend time examining the various possibilities to look at the best method possible to overcome them and help the student achieve their best. To become an emotionally intelligent leader of people we need to manage ourselves as well as understand others. Getting the best from others means getting the best from them as they are, not as you imagine or want them to be.*

» *Your leadership style will develop well if you are able to set your own vision, understand what motivates you and why you think as you do, as well as being able to share a vision with others in an inspiring way and then, on top of all that, knowing the kind of people that you are going to lead, taking into account the factors that have brought them here. The greatest teachers are those who are willing to learn from those they teach.*

Next steps

We have spent a good deal of time looking at how we develop as humans and the influence of those developments on what makes us unique individuals. We will now look in the next chapter at what we can do to make the classroom environment work most effectively for us as we examine what an emotionally intelligent classroom looks like.

Taking it further

Belbin® www.belbin.com

Myers & Briggs MBTI® www.myersbriggs.org

Take a psychometric test and read and evaluate the findings to get a better understanding of yourself. Discuss the finding with a trusted friend or colleague. Consider the areas that are highlighted regarding your preferred work environment and think about how you can encourage your students to recognise what is required of them within your classroom by discussing these findings. Often, if your preferred working environment is one of calm, then too much noise will raise your anxiety levels, yet another colleague may thrive on noise. Highlight, through your greater understanding, what you are looking for and why, but be aware that for some students this may not come easy.

www.opp.com/ is the European distributor of the MBTI®. They offer training courses on understanding the implications of the MBTI® in the workplace, on conflict and team building. They also train facilitators of the MBTI® and coach people in understanding the results of individual tests.

References

Briggs Myers, I (1995) *Gifts Differing: Understanding Personality Type*. Mountain View, CA: Davies-Black Publishing.

Jung, C G (1923) *Psychological Types: Or the Psychology of Individuation*. Oxford: Harcourt, Brace.

Townsend, R (2007) *Up the Organization: How to Stop the Corporation from Stifling People and Strangling Profits*. Hoboken, NJ: Jossey-Bass.

Wimbrow, D (1934) *The Guy in the Glass*. Online: www.theguyintheglass.com/gig.htm (last accessed 29 May 2018).

4 The emotionally intelligent classroom

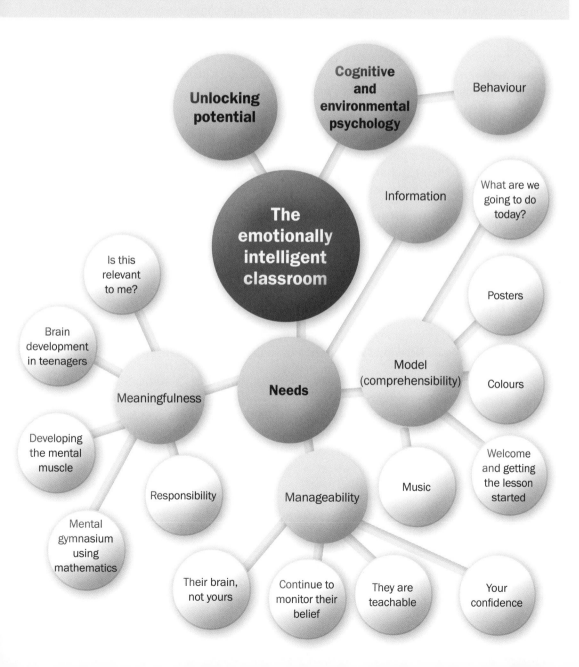

Introduction

Where are you while you are reading this chapter? What place have you decided is conducive to reading? Is there music in the background, or is it quiet? Are there any distractions and are you having to shut them out or are you in a private place so that the book can hold your attention without distraction? Are you outside, or in your bed? How warm are you? What things have you done to prepare yourself for reading to help you learn?

Are you, as you read this book, processing the information to see how it fits into your life? Is it making sense to you? Are you assessing it against what you already know? Are you excited at the possibility of learning new things or confirming things you already know? Are you thinking about how you can use this information in your career and future?

These two areas of questioning are the two areas I want to look at in this chapter. They are concerned with the mental preparedness of your students as well as the environmental factors that you can influence while they are with you.

In the previous chapters we have looked at some issues that your students may have faced that will have influenced their lives as well as what will be happening to them while you have them with you through a period of years. We have also looked at the motivational factors that caused you to be their teacher, what your vision is for them as you seek to instruct, guide and teach them in the years ahead.

We will look at aspects of cognitive and environmental psychology, the natural influences that enable us to learn and contribute in an encouraging and supportive manner. We will look at your classroom and what you can do to make it into an emotionally intelligent place for all to learn and contribute.

Cognitive and environmental psychology

The term cognitive psychology was first used in 1967 by American psychologist Ulric Neisser in his book *Cognitive Psychology*. According to Neisser, cognition involves

> all processes by which the sensory input is transformed, reduced, elaborated, stored, recovered, and used. It is concerned with these processes even when they operate in the absence of relevant stimulation, as in images and hallucinations... Given such a sweeping definition, it is apparent that cognition is involved in everything a human being might possibly do; that every psychological phenomenon is a cognitive phenomenon.
>
> (Neisser, 1967, p 4)

The core focus of cognitive psychology is on how people acquire, process and store information. Environmental psychology builds upon this idea that as a species we are driven to find and process information and use it to make sense of our world. With this in mind, we are fully aware that the environment in which we find ourselves provides us with information with which to make judgements as well as motivating us to make decisions. Findings from both these areas of psychology help us build a platform on which to create an environment, both physical and mental, that will be beneficial for all those we teach and that will have an impact upon the behaviour as well as the well-being of our students.

The term environment, therefore, is more than just the physical aspects of our surroundings, it includes all aspects in which we are processing information. So we need to be conscious that everything we do will have an impact on those we come into contact with as we have become a part of their environment, and that the environment we create or influence can have either an empowering or debilitating effect on others. There may be things that you can control as well as things that you cannot. For example, an unusually windy day may cause some students a problem when it comes to settling down. At other times, the temperature in the room may be too hot or too cold to work.

Behaviour

We have already noted that the behaviour perceived as unreasonable within a classroom may come from a variety of sources and requires us to look at possible causes. We have also previously looked at things we can do or say that may help the student cope better with the situation in which they find themselves.

Environmental psychologists Rachel and Stephen Kaplan suggest that the differences between reasonable and unreasonable behaviour may also be partly explained by the environment in which people find themselves. They base this observation upon the fact that we humans have a remarkable facility to process information and that the information that we process has a very close relationship with the effect it has on us.

Needs

The questions I asked you at the start of the chapter targeted your information gathering into specific areas, such as your immediate climate, as well as your future life. You are able to process those thoughts while reading, and while reading you are still gathering related information: is the noise level still conducive to reading? Can I manage to stay focused? Is the atmosphere too hot or is it getting cold? Am I hungry or thirsty? (Sorry if I have just made you consider getting a drink while you are reading.) All the time, you are processing information and this information will be evaluated against your model of informational needs (Kaplan and Kaplan, 2005).

Information

Before looking at these needs, it might be helpful to look at what Kaplan (1995) points out about information: we are information-based organisms, *'we yearn for it, we hoard it, we are overwhelmed by it, we trade it, we hide it. We ask questions such as "How do I get there?" "How does that thing work?" and "What happened?"'*

Information is all around us in its many forms and we are processing vast amounts of information all the time, eg the noise, the layout of a room, other people and their behaviours, things we encounter and events unfolding in front of us, all impact upon us all the time and we do our best to make sense of it all. As reflected on in earlier chapters, our basic survival has grown out of the necessity to make sense of what is around us, how it is impacting us and what we need to do in relation to the things we are discovering.

This basic model is now understood to contain three categories of informational need for us to function in a reasonable way.

I call this the 3 Ms: Model, Manageable, and Meaningful. These three parts are being monitored within the lives of us all every moment of the day. If any one or mixture of them is out of kilter with what we can manage or understand then we will begin to get stressed and seek for ways to bring them back within our understanding. If I ever have to go and carry out a lesson observation and young people or students are not on task it will be one or more of these three reasons. If any one of these is out of line with you then you will experience anxiety. Keeping these things in line with every one of your students will require you to know them and build relationships with them. If any student is in need of a talk with you then I would advise you to ask them about these three items to see how they respond as they will be your starting point.

1. Model (comprehensibility): things have to make sense to us, and we do this by evaluating all that we see and experience around us with an internal model of what we think things should be like and expect them to be. This will help us manage day-to-day experiences. The way in which the things we are experiencing link in with our understanding and our model will affect how well we cope, as well as how we are feeling.

2. Manageability: this affects our belief in ourselves as to how effective and competent we are to cope with what we have to do, in changing situations. To bring out our best, we have to feel capable and competent.

3. Meaningfulness: we have to feel that what we are doing is meaningful, not only for us but also for the world in which we participate. We like to feel respected, valued and recognised for our contribution, and we like to think we can make a difference in the long run and that what we are doing has some relevance to our own lives.

These three factors will manifest themselves within your lessons, and how quickly and consistently you can manage them will determine your success in maintaining a calm environment conducive to learning. We will look at these in more detail now and examine what you can do to monitor and assess how well you are doing.

Model (comprehensibility)

What are we going to do today?

You will often be asked this question at the start of the lesson. The reason for this is that the student has arrived at your class and everything is how they expect it to be. As they have experienced in the past, things are in order, you are there, you are welcoming them, others have arrived, the timetable is working, it's the right time. The mental model is all in place, yet the one thing that is still missing is the information about what is now going to happen. They need this answered before they can move on to the next stage, which will be to assess their part in it.

So what can you do to make sure that, first of all, the things that they have assessed create for them a picture of calmness and preparedness to learn? Think back to how they arrive, because all the processes that have become the norm will also be impacting upon them and affecting how they conduct themselves. A disorganised start will lead to a disorganised lesson. A stern start will dictate the attitude of learning. A telling-off brings out a defensive nature. A reminder of misdemeanours harks back to their attitude and behaviour from the last time. That is why it's important to start with positives and with fresh expectations because the things that needed dealing with have been dealt with and an opportunity to prove themselves capable has introduced itself.

But this is looking at what things are like within a term. I want you to consider the fresh start; this is the way things are going to be from now on. This is the model that you want them to start building on in their minds. What do you want them to be thinking about as they make their way to your class?

Critical questions

» *What does your classroom look like? Get the mental model right.*

» *Have you got used to things that you didn't like when you first arrived?*

» *Have you ever asked a colleague their first impressions as they walk in?*

» *What does it say about you?*

I have sometimes gone into a classroom and the teacher's first words to me are *'Well this is it, sorry about the mess. I have been meaning to clear it away but never got around to it.'*

They have just helped me with my model of them and it's not a favourable one. I know that you shouldn't judge a book by its cover, but we do. Young people are constantly judging people by what they see and how they are made to feel, and they won't be able to alter what they are initially processing subconsciously into something more favourable.

A messy classroom will affect those who have to work in it, just as a messy, cluttered staffroom will affect the staff, just as a messy and cluttered lecture hall will affect you as you have to sit and listen to a lecture.

Get things in order, even if you are, like me, someone who if they cannot see something then they don't know where it is. Yet I know that my office and any classroom I work in has to be clutter free, as I need the students' mental models to take the environment for granted, so they don't have to think about it but can focus upon what I need them to be focusing on.

Just as you need to consider what you don't want there, you also need to be thinking about what you do want.

Posters

Displaying posters outlining expectations of classroom behaviour or of your students' work creates a very strong backdrop to your lessons. Posters will make an instant and enduring impression on all those in the classroom, so it is very important to ensure that they convey the messages you want them to.

Critical questions

» What posters or work do you want to display?

» What signs, information or encouraging messages do you want to include?

» How often do you change them and how often do you draw the students' attention to them? Remember that every comment that you make about them will be replayed in their minds every time the students look at them again.

» What do the posters say about social skills as well as academic achievement?

Colours

Most classrooms are painted a very neutral colour, yet it has been noticed that colour affects mood; even if the link and effect is only temporary, you want the first impression to set the mental model that will become the norm. Think of calming, relaxing colours such as blues and greens, and pictures of nature; it has been noticed that posters of forests and landscapes can help with the healing process for patients within hospitals so should have some effect upon students within your classroom to add to the calm and learning mood.

Music

My daughter Esther recently did her dissertation about the calming effect that music has within the classroom. In her findings, she noticed that students found it helpful to listen to classical or non-vocal music as it helped with their capacity to stay focused. This may have something to do with the fact that the mind needs to be constantly processing the environment. If music thus takes up a good portion of their attention, students are less distracted by other things and are able to target their attention more effectively.

Music can be used in a variety of ways and I am a strong believer that it should play more of a role within lessons and not just in a few where it has to be a part, such as Music and Drama.

Why not play appropriate period music in a history lesson or an English lesson? Music can help set a scene and create a mood, and it is such a part of our lives outside the classroom that it's a shame not to use it within the classroom. Esther Allen did find that current and up-to-date music was too much of a distraction as it led to comments and disagreements, so it is important to keep it neutral and calming.

Critical questions

» What music would be appropriate and related to the topic you are covering?

» Could you use music to regulate noise control?

» Can you link your music to the music department curriculum?

Welcome and getting the lesson started

How you welcome your students into the classroom and a seating plan are two things that can work in your favour. I am an advocate of seating plans for only two reasons:

1. to help you remember students' names;

2. to group your class together according to ability and learning.

I don't agree with moving students when they are unable to stop talking with their friends – as I have mentioned, this is a learning opportunity, to help them develop emotional intelligence. Moving them takes away an opportunity for them to develop a skill and will in fact perpetuate their poor behaviour. We will look at what can be done later in the book.

So the first area to consider is the physical environment in which you are playing your part by welcoming them and being ready for them. It is a good idea to have them lined up outside before letting them come into the classroom as this helps them understand that the space they are entering is yours, they have to be invited into it and they have to do so on your terms. It is also a chance for you to comment approvingly on their behaviour or dress and also to pass on to them your pleasure in seeing them again. Regardless of what or how you are feeling, it's important that you are creating the right model for them.

The question 'What are we going to do today?' can be covered in a number of ways. Information could be on the board with simple outlines, or you could set the first slide to have a specific coloured background, eg blue for a new topic, green for revision, red for a quiz and review.

When teachers have used this technique they have said that incidences of students asking them what they are going to do have significantly reduced and also that the students have been quicker at getting started once the instructions have been given.

Critical questions

» *Do you have a consistent entry into your class?*

» *Have you developed a strategy for remembering names?*

» *What can you do to introduce the topic instantly on arrival?*

» *How welcoming are you?*

Overall, the atmosphere that you create at the start needs to be one that the students get used to as they will be approaching your lesson with that model in mind, and if it's disorganised, late starting or inconstant in approach then the lesson will also contain elements of that within it. However hard it is to establish a routine that may be unfamiliar to the students, it will be harder not doing so. The problems that you may have to start with are just them trying to make it fit with what they have been used to or what is familiar to them. Over time, your method and approach will become the norm and it's then that you will reap the reward. It may take weeks, but it will be worth it. Remember to keep calm, polite, encouraging and consistent throughout, as this will speed up the process. You may also feel you are not supported by colleagues who don't have routines or follow procedures and the students may point out to you that others don't do the same. Again, this is just the students trying to make sense of the situation and to build for themselves a model that they understand, so it is enough for you to say, *'Well, with me, this is what I want for my classroom, so that we can all learn together.'* You can only be responsible for your own place to start with, so that is where you should start, and how you tackle issues will be the best method for encouraging others to do likewise.

Manageability

I can't do that! I love that!

Once you have outlined to the students what they will be doing, they quickly process that information to see if they are able to manage it. So this is the next stage that you need to bear in mind as you want to keep them with a positive mental model.

For those who are telling you that they can't do it or that it's something that they hate or don't like doing, please don't just dismiss this comment with a casual *'yes you can'*, or *'well, you just have to get on with it'* or even, *'there's lots of things I don't like doing but I have to get on with it'*. These are all comments that I have heard and all go some way in highlighting how the teacher is feeling but they don't help a lot towards what the student is feeling. So what should you do? Well, you need to acknowledge that their feeling is real and valid and that you are giving them the attention because of what they are feeling by addressing the issue.

For some, I have encouraged them to ask the question of the whole class by asking, *'Who doesn't feel they can do this or who feels it is really too hard?'* This is your time to help them see that, even if they are going to find it hard, you are going to help them overcome the difficulty and they won't have to do it alone. Emphasise that you are going to be there with them every step of the way along the road to discovery.

Imagine that you have to do something that you worry about and that you know is going to be very hard – not impossible but outside your comfort zone. Think of how many times you mention it to your friends or colleagues or members of your family. You are subconsciously looking for moral support. When you get this support, it helps towards confronting or dealing with the situation. We need to feel capable and competent, and when we don't feel either of those things, we are not working at our best. So if a student isn't feeling capable or competent then they, too, will be going through a period of anxiety and their repertoire of coping methods will be drastically reduced, which may be enough for them to start their disruptive behaviour.

As we have seen, students will be doing things that help them manage the situation in which they find themselves. On occasions, this may involve avoidance techniques and, especially if they feel anxious about a particular lesson, they may not attend. If students are persistently absent, then it is worth asking whether they are avoiding a particular lesson as it may have something to do with their feeling of inadequacy when it comes to that lesson.

What can you do to avoid the issue or at least make it less anxiety-producing for the students who have highlighted that they are feeling unsure about their ability in the subject?

Critical questions

»   *How many times do you check the emotional comfort of the class?*

»   *Do you check the confidence of the students when introducing a new topic?*

Your confidence

Inspire confidence at all times and in all situations. If you can master this ability you will go a long way to reducing the anxiety of the people you are going to teach. To have someone who knows what they are doing helping you or taking charge changes how you feel towards the event, no matter what the situation.

From the outset, you need to establish your credentials and, if possible, demonstrate how competent you are. For example, I often ask music teachers to play the instrument with which they are most competent, if possible. This resulted in one music teacher using the piano to take his lessons, using the tempo and music to lighten the mood. It was a pleasure to attend the registration as he greeted them with a very upbeat tune, sometimes mimicking how he thought they were feeling. And throughout the lesson, he kept using the music to demonstrate how the lesson was going and to help them either speed up or take care, playing gently to keep the volume down, just short snippets but enough to make music a part of the time with him.

Another music teacher used a baton to conduct the behaviour of the class and regulate the speed and volume level. She introduced the idea by showing clips of various conductors, explaining what she was expecting from them just as a conductor would for an orchestra. She pointed out how the players concentrated on their instrument but kept checking with the conductor that they were on track, and that was what she wanted them to do while doing their work. A couple of taps on the table and they all got used to paying attention.

Language teachers could speak the language as often as they can, especially between other language teachers. Demonstrate that the language you are teaching is useful and relevant. After these exchanges sometimes ask the students what they think they have been speaking about. This helps them see that understanding the language starts with understanding a few words and making connections.

For the mathematics teacher, show the extent of what you are able to work out and master. Whatever your subject, find a way of demonstrating your mastery of it or even just your ability to try in it. Even if it's not your first subject, this is still important to help your students know that you are worth listening to as you know what you are talking about.

CASE STUDY

I recently asked an art teacher which of the art on display within the classroom was hers, and she said, 'I'm not that good and don't think it's worth showing.' We then talked about the times that she has to talk to students who say exactly the same thing. Your attitude and confidence will affect your students, as will any lack of confidence that you demonstrate. She brought in her art and started to display not only what she had done during her university days but also what she was working on at the time. This led to her exhibiting her work along with the students' work, which helped the parents see the excellence and ability of the teacher as well, and helped them see that their child's advancement was in the hands of someone very competent.

Critical questions

» *In what ways can you demonstrate your mastery of the subject?*

» *How can you demonstrate your competence of the subject in a related way of life? I had an accounts teacher who could do mental arithmetic faster than I could on a calculator. I was impressed enough to think he is good at his subject and enjoys it.*

They are teachable

No matter what level of competence they are at, let them also know that you are familiar with their situation and that you have the skills to help them learn and develop competence within the subject. After asking them about their feelings towards the subject and their belief in their own ability, tell those who have said that they don't think they can or know that they are useless that you will spend special time with them as you take delight in being able to help people overcome problems, and if they really are sure they can't do it then that is even better for you as you will enjoy helping them even more. Point out that it's important that they work with you and together you will both be able to succeed. Remember to listen to what they are saying and not dismiss their fears and negativity but to use their words as the starting position on which to build.

Continue to monitor their belief

Each lesson will be a new start and it's important that you continually monitor their own personal belief in their understanding and competence. This is also an excellent way of helping develop co-operation between students by encouraging them to share new-found knowledge and understanding with those who are finding it difficult. The best way to embed new learning is to teach it to someone else.

CASE STUDY

Checking confidence

A very quick and simple check of students' confidence is, at the start of the lesson when you have established with the class what the learning objectives are, to ask them to stand at various places in the room dependent upon either their understanding or their confidence in learning the subject. Sometimes I have seen this done by asking both questions as it helps the teacher see that lack of confidence has the ability to stunt the ability to learn. So, after you have ascertained their understanding and ability, you can either set those who are more confident to work with those with less confidence, or you can set those who are very confident a harder task to stretch them, while you spend some time with the more anxious students. You can ask the same question again during the lesson to see who has moved (hopefully in a positive way) and again at the end to check that all have indeed made progress.

Their brain, not yours

When you are having to spend time with a student who is having difficulty learning a new topic or struggling to understand, a good rule of thumb is not to stay with them for more than 15 seconds at a time. By then, you should have been able to ascertain either that your explanation might have caused confusion and perhaps needs to be restated to the whole class or that they might be paired with someone who has overcome the point on which they are struggling. Any longer and they are starting to use your brain more than their own. Asking simple questions to find at what point they started to struggle and making key comments to unlock the problem should be all that is required. It is too easy for some teachers to get into the position of sharing their own knowledge and understanding rather than being facilitators of the students' learning.

Critical questions

»   *What words do you use to demonstrate your belief in their ability in a way that they can relate to?*

»   *How can you start to enlist the help of other students to pass on their knowledge to struggling students?*

»   *How long do you typically help any one student?*

»   *Do you spend equal time on your students or have some become more time consuming?*

»   *What are your alternatives within the class if this is the case?*

Once you have overcome the first two aspects that help to make a relaxed model to work within, the final part is meaningfulness.

Meaningfulness

Is this relevant to me?

Out of the three, this is the most important and should always be your starting point if any issues occur. What is relevant to the person you are talking to? Once you have found this out and then linked it to what they are doing, they will find ways to manage it. If it is not relevant what is the point of engaging with it? Sometimes we try to help a person manage and find strategies to cope or work through a problem without finding out if they actually see any relevance in doing it. This will always end in frustration not only for those trying but also to those helping.

I remember talking with a student who was outside a humanities lesson who said, '*I am not going to be a vicar so why should I learn about religion?*'

Alongside the first question that we mentioned ('*what are we doing today?*') and the comments associated with it ('*I am no good*' or '*that's good*') goes the question that you will inevitably hear during your teaching career: '*why are we learning this?*'

The following are typical answers I have heard that don't help.

- The government tells us to teach it.

- This is what you need for your exam.

- It's on the syllabus.

- You will need this if you want to get a good job.

The reason these answers don't help is that they don't address the issue that is actually relevant to the students in the situation of having to give the subject their undivided attention for the next hour. Remember that the front part of the brain that deals with forward planning isn't yet mature. They have difficulty knowing what they are going to do at the weekend, let alone what they are planning on doing in a few years' time, so university is a long long way off and so is getting a job. For a lot of them, the most pressing issue that they have to face is how am I going to handle the next hour in front of me with my peers around me? How is what I have to do next going to give me a sense of purpose and add value to my life? This is why they ask the questions because the answers that they have come up with themselves haven't satisfied them, so they are asking you. If your answer does not satisfy them either, they will not want to engage. Over the course of the lesson, they will demonstrate to you that they are not interested and no amount of warnings or detentions will shift them from feeling that it is a waste of their time. They may comply to some extent, but it will be grudgingly, and the amount of work that will be produced will be minimal and of low quality. It is not enough for you to think that it's not your fault because you don't see the point for them either. You have to find the answer to the question and get that answer to fit in with where your students are in their lives.

Think about how much easier it is to be involved in something when you can be clear-headed about it and understand its context and relevance. It is even better if you know that the part you are playing will have a lasting effect upon yourself and others around you.

As a species, we like to make a difference. We like to leave our mark on the world and be remembered. This can also be understood by those who just want to leave their personal tag on a building or who want to look back and remember any contribution that had an effect, from the first cave paintings to the latest book or post on Twitter.

Responsibility

This is why sometimes giving responsibility to a student who often misbehaves works well, as the student has been given a sense of worth and purpose that was lacking before. They have to feel respected and this is hard for them if they feel inadequate or incompetent. Therefore your involvement and encouragement will be a powerful tool. Any comment that belittles them or undermines their work will have far-reaching effects that will take a long time to repair. It isn't just the comment that is affecting them, it is the model in their minds that you have now created that they will remember every time they meet you or hear about you.

You have to know the answer to the question, *'What difference is this lesson going to make in the life of the student?'* Once that has been established, then the rest can be worked at, so it is important that, at the start of each new period of learning, you clarify the importance of the subject of your lesson within the lives of the students.

I use two methods when the topic cannot be seen to have a relevant impact on students' lives. Mathematics is often seen as a class that students struggle in and give up on. They don't see the point of learning formulas or trying to discover the elusive x.

Mental gymnasium using mathematics

Most students understand the relevance of exercise; they know about press-ups and squat thrusts. They have heard of a bench press and some have even tried it. I ask them how many they can do of any of these exercises and then I talk to them about a personal trainer who is there to help them develop muscles and get them to do more when they feel like giving up. The reason that they are doing the exercises isn't so that they can do more bench presses or sit-ups, as those are not relevant within any job they are doing, but having done them does have an effect upon their fitness and health, which will impact upon their job and general life.

It's the same with mathematics. The relevance of learning a formula or the ability to know how to find x may never play a part in later life, but in working out the answer, the brain, like a muscle, will become fitter and more able to cope in life, and will become quicker at processing things and more skilled at multi-tasking and dealing with stress.

Developing the mental muscle

I therefore encourage mathematics teachers to help the students see that mathematics class is the mental gymnasium of the school making the brain stronger and fitter. I suggest that in some lessons the teacher describes the difficulty of a problem by appointing kilos to it and asking who thinks they have the mental capacity to lift it.

The teacher becomes the personal trainer within the lesson and the students get used to knowing that they will find some things hard and they will struggle, but such is life and those are no reasons to give up.

Brain development in teenagers

This brings me to the second method. I tell students about the development of their brain, that it is still a work in progress and that it is developing itself into a tool that they will use for the rest of their life, as we looked at earlier. But I emphasise that, for them, it is still in the development stage and it is trying to find optimum working patterns and that they can help it develop. They can train it to give in or they can train it to work through tough times.

I try to show them that school teaches more than subjects; it teaches them how to handle life. If they are going to use school effectively they need to see the lessons for what they are – a time to develop their ability to manage their adult life and to handle things that life will give them.

Those are two methods I have used that have worked when students have not seen the relevance of the subject, and I head back to those points time and time again with them and ask them how their ability to persevere is developing.

Unlocking potential

As an educator you are there to help unlock the potential of the students. When you manage to answer with satisfaction those three areas within a student's mind so that they can build a mental model that makes sense to them, you will go a long way to having a classroom where students are engaged and learning, and issues that cause anxiety and stress are reduced, leading to reasonable behaviour. Remember that in each new class that you go into you will have already disrupted the first part of the model, comprehensibility; you have become a change for them. It is not the change that is difficult, it is more that you are not yet familiar to them, so you have to appreciate that it will inevitably take time for them to adjust and get used to you. Consistency is the key over this period. That is why, even if you have become familiar and accepted, a long-term absence will change the model, and you will no longer be familiar, so you need to rebuild that model.

The way that you manage and lead your class will say a lot about who you are and will be something that you will develop and hone over the years. Figure 4.1 is a checklist of things to monitor relating to an emotionally intelligent classroom to assist you in keeping a check on things that are important. It should be used along with the pattern of delivery mentioned above, and together they will help you to become an excellent teacher, knowing that you are laying a firm foundation that will support students emotionally on which you can build academic success. In the figure, FE denotes 'fully embedded', S denotes 'strength' and ES denotes 'emerging strength'.

Figure 4.1 Classroom culture

Classroom culture	Student	Teacher	FE	S	ES
1. Belonging	• Smiling and feels welcome in the class • Co-operative and willing to 'have a go' • Appears relaxed but attentive • Good relationships with teachers and other students • Wants to be in class • Enjoys learning	• Smiling / teacher warmth / positive relationship • Greet at the door / use personal hooks to engage students • Positive body language • Knowing your class / students / 'cueing' in by name • Tone of voice is appropriate to maintain inclusive climate • Class seating / arrangement • Whole class encouragement ongoing			
2. Accessibility	• Understands learning intentions • Knows what to do to improve • Knows how to gain help • Comfortable in the environment • Understands the relevance of the lesson • Has made it meaningful for themselves	• Differentiated resources • Clarity of expected outcomes • Effective use of additional adults • Illuminated seating plans • Teacher checks for understanding of vocabulary and instructions • Teacher models effectively, using clear explanations • Tidy, ordered classroom • Provided relevant purpose to the class on the topic			
3. Engagement in learning	• Punctual to lessons • Student asks and answers questions • Attentive • Enthusiastic learner	• Open questioning pitched to challenge • TIF – Take it further strategies deployed • Teacher enthusiasm / humour • Targeted questioning / time is given for response • Different communication methods	FE	S	ES

Classroom culture	Student	Teacher	FE	S	ES
4. Confidence/ self-esteem	• Contributes in class • Takes risks • Not afraid to make mistakes • Takes pride in work • Feels challenged but is not panicked	• Teacher patience • Think / pair / share – talk for learning • Scaffolding to assist tasks • Checks for understanding • Use of praise and reward for emotional social as well as academic progress			
5. Resilience	• Stays on task • Manages distractions • Perseveres • Regulates emotions • Can reflect on work and behaviour • Regular redrafting of work	• Unstuck strategies • Teacher encouragement that reinforcing tenacity • Failure is acceptable			
6. Ambitious for success	• Students involved in setting criteria • Student shows they can work independently • Student take responsibility • There is a desire to achieve • Targets are actioned • Home learning is completed • Students have goals linked to personal vision	• Appropriate positive behaviour noticed • Acknowledgement of success • High expectations are shared • Student's work matters and is valued • Bespoke targets for improvement are set and responded to			

CASE STUDY

Year 8, Mayville High School, Portsmouth

It has been a pleasure to work with Victor and embark in what is proving to be one of the most exciting journeys we have had in education so far. Becoming an emotional intelligent school has enabled us to reflect upon the very important role we play in children's lives and how we can best equip them for a changing world in which they will thrive as rounded individuals. Victor has run two inset training sessions with us to embed our knowledge on brain development and maintaining our own emotion when dealing with others.

In this case study we have focused on the Year 8 cohort as they seem to be finding their identity, no longer being the young one new to Senior School with all the attention and understanding from teachers, yet not Year 9 with all the perceived challenges that they face and that we all seem to be ready for.

We would describe our Year 8 as a typical Year 8 cohort, with some friendship issues, particularly among girls and some silly behaviour from the boys.

As spring term was beginning, teachers noticed that behaviour issues seemed to kick in – hormones changing, falling outs, lack of focus in class and lack of energy around the school. Thanks to Victor we now know that this is due to brain development!

Our positive working party met and discussed what we could do to move matters forward and all agreed that it would be beneficial to trial some sessions with the entire cohort... and what a fantastic response we had from pupils and staff!

Starting with an assembly explaining what happens to our brains as we develop, Year 8 started to understand why some of the behaviour was happening and how challenging this time can be for them as well as for the people around them. However, it was important to us that we also stressed that we were aware that this was happening and wished to help them. Our wish was to coach each individual through what can be a challenging time in their lives. We made it clear that we were not here to judge, but rather to help them reflect upon their behaviour and understand how in every situation they had choices. This seemed to empower them very much.

Pupils were given the opportunity to talk about they feel in school, what they struggle with and ultimately how we, the staff, could help them in their journey at school. We promised to allow some sessions for them to think as a team and come up with some ideas and strategies, which would then be shared with all staff. We stressed again that all staff were there here to listen and help them!

Year 8 took matters very seriously and came up with a list of things that we could do to help them. Here are some of their suggestions.

1.   Staff to be aware of their emotional intelligence. (We absolutely love this one. How can we coach pupils in becoming emotionally intelligent if we are not aware of our emotions and how to deal with them?)

2.   Do not shout but talk to us.

3.   Do not single out pupils who are struggling, rather help them

4.   Give people who struggle a buddy who is emotionally intelligent.

We emailed all staff and asked for us all to work together to support Year 8. Equally, our Year 8 pupils are aware that staff will have high expectations, they will ask for respect and follow the 3 Ms in every lesson.

We have spent the past month working with them and we surely can notice the difference. More focus in class, pupils helping one another, having mature conversations with staff, taking responsibility for their actions and most importantly for us, understanding and having empathy for pupils who struggle at times.

Pupils do wish to do well, they do wish to be part of a team, and they need to see where they are going and why. During our PSHE lessons we reinforce these messages of belonging, purpose and empathy, and will continue to do so. Every so often we visit our Year 8 pupils, praising them, talking to them about how things are going, and this makes them happy as they feel they belong, they feel we care about them as a group and as individuals. The journey is not at the end by any means. There is so much more we can and will do to support them because they matter. We have a huge responsibility as staff to ensure they have the best care while they are with us so that they can grow into splendid human beings, both emotionally and intellectually.

Critical questions

» *How can you relate what you are teaching to the students' lives?*

» *How can you help them become personally involved in the positive outcome of the lesson?*

» *How well do you know your students to enable you to target an appropriate answer to why are we doing this?*

» *What aspects of the current world situations relate to what is being taught?*

Chapter reflections

» *We have taken a look at how the subconscious mind is processing information the whole time and will be the trigger for how the student is going to react from one moment to the next. There are things that you can do to create and maintain a good working environment, but it is important that these things are continually monitored to help students stay focused and on task.*

» *You also need to take into account the students' personality and this will require you getting to know them, so that they feel valued as individuals. Over time, you can experiment with what works and what is best suited for the types of lessons that you are teaching.*

» *Always take into account the three things that are continually being processed (model, manageability and meaningfulness) and when things go astray, try to pinpoint the areas where you had become weak.*

» *To make sure that your lessons are always relevant, look at your subject as a whole and create a life-journey highway, highlighting crucial chapters in a person's life when that specific subject knowledge is going to prove to be invaluable.*

» *Remember, the work of a teacher is to make everything else in life accessible and possible.*

Taking it further

Eysenck, M and Keane, MT (2010) *Cognitive Psychology: A Student's Handbook*. Hove, UK: Psychology Press.

References

Kaplan, R (1995) Informational Issues: A Perspective on Human Needs and Inclinations, in Bradley, G A (ed) *Urban Forest Landscapes: Integrating Multidisciplinary Perspectives* (pp 60–71). Seattle: University of Washington Press.

Kaplan, R and Kaplan, S (2005) Preference, Restoration, and Meaningful Action in the Context of Nearby Nature, in Barlett, P F (ed) *Urban Place: Reconnecting with the Natural World* (pp 271–98). Cambridge, MA: MIT Press.

Neisser, U (1967) *Cognitive Psychology*. New York: Appleton-Century-Crofts.

5 The right BASE

Classroom climate — Autonomy — Method

Belonging (relatedness) — The right BASE

Self-esteem (social and emotional competence)

Building a community — Building self-worth — Topcliffe Primary School, Birmingham

Introduction

The basic psychological needs for human growth and development are:

- **B**elonging;

- **A**utonomy; and

- **S**elf-**E**steem (through Social and Emotional competence).

Hence 'BASE'.

The academic grounding of this approach can be found in Connell and Wellborn (1991), Deci et al (1991) and Ryan (1995) if you'd like to investigate further. For the purposes of this book, I have adapted the approach to make it memorable and easy to apply within any setting.

You probably read and hear a lot about young people and stress, and also the lack of connectedness they feel. Young people often feel a lack of control, being part of situations going on around them which they feel they can play little or no part in, even if such situations can have a serious impact upon their own lives. In many schools there are students joining who have travelled from various parts of the globe, to find a home in Great Britain. In one class I asked a teacher how many nationalities he was teaching, and we counted ten.

No matter what situation your learners find themselves in and no matter where on the planet they have come from, the three basic needs for human growth (BASE) will always be the same. This book looks at these in more detail as they provide the foundation on which to build everything else that you might seek to do. If you get this right, along with following the 3 Ms, you will have what is needed to build mentally strong, mentally capable learners. This approach could be especially effective with more vulnerable members of your classes. It's vital that you get the BASE right, which also means taking into account the emotional and social learning that young people have experienced as they grew up.

I want to stress that this is not just related to the young people whom you are aiming to teach but will also include yourself and other members of your team, as well as other staff. We continually look for and find our own identity in who we are with others and within the emotional atmosphere of a school.

The satisfaction of each of these BASE needs affects psychological development and the overall experiences of well-being and health, even if we are not aware of them (Ryan, 1995). When students and young people's needs are not satisfied in educational settings, Deci et al (1991) predict diminished responsibility, impaired development, alienation and poor performance. If these behaviours start to emerge within a young person, what inevitably happens is that schools look to putting into place alternative lessons and extra support outside of the normal classroom. Unfortunately, even though these strategies may be well intentioned, I believe they add to the lack of a sense of belonging within the classroom and school, lower the person's ability to feel good about themselves, and can take away their autonomy.

This is why once a young person has been provided with support it usually means they will stay with that support through most of their school life, and that they will probably find it increasingly difficult to return to the normal structure of lessons.

We should start by looking at the person's sense of belonging. This means looking at what their teachers do to create for them an environment where they belong. It is so important to build that up as soon as a young person comes into contact with you and the school.

There is enough evidence to show that the sense of belonging is associated with difference in cognitive process, emotional patterns, behaviour, health and well-being, which affects people's perceptions of others, leading people to view friends and group members more favourably.

Being accepted, included or welcomed leads to positive emotions, such as happiness, elation, contentment and calm; while being rejected, excluded or ignored leads to often intense negative feelings of anxiety, depression, grief, jealousy and loneliness. A lack of belongingness is also associated with incidences of mental and physical illness and a broad range of behavioural problems. I believe that we have underestimated how important this is within the life of schools.

The next chapter provides you with strategies to use with students and young people within your class, but also within this chapter we look at getting the BASE right for their cognitive development and engagement. This should always come first.

Let's look in more detail at how to ensure you lay that foundation and create the right BASE for all you aim to teach.

Belonging (relatedness)

The term relatedness is a psychological concept that parallels a sense of acceptance and belonging.

Within the first few seconds of meeting someone you are processing so many things about them. Your interaction has the ability to impact upon their emotions. You can easily make a young person feel better or worse about themselves and the mood which is created can stay with the other person for a long time. Just think of the time when someone made you feel bad. How long did it take for you to get over that emotion?

Someone entering your classroom needs to feel good about meeting you, from the very moment they meet you. When you are confronted with a large new group of young people and students for the first time, the first thing you will need to do is spend time getting to know them, to allow them to get to know about you and about each other.

I mentioned that I have written a mental security programme which is being used within schools and works through the entire school year. This process starts with getting to know others. You are wanting everyone within your classroom to start thinking of themselves as a team, and the sooner you can create this the better things will go for you. It is also the start of providing them with a life skill that will prove useful throughout their lives. Companies understand the importance of developing leaders and teams, recognising that this works towards effectiveness and efficiency. This is also what you are aiming to build within your classroom.

CASE STUDY

I was asked by a PE teacher to visit her tutor group as she was having difficulties with low-level disturbance and lack of engagement. I asked her what she does when she has a PE lesson for the first time, and she described some of the team-building games she employs to help the students appreciate how much better it is if they work together. When asked if she had done the same with her tutor group, she realised she hadn't, and when she thought about it, couldn't understand why she hadn't done so. Her next tutor sessions all started with short classroom-based 'get to know each other' team-building games. At the end of a few weeks she had what she wanted, a class working together.

Ask students to share three things about themselves and you can lead by example. Remind them to keep it positive and about things they like. It is often easier for some to focus upon the negative but to begin with you want to keep it positive; those negative aspects can be addressed at another time.

Sharing common aims and a common vision is also key to building teams and a sense of belonging. Asking your students to think about what they want to achieve through the coming year is also a great way of getting them to think about themselves and what they wish to develop or who they wish to be. This can include anything within their lives personally as well as educational aims.

When talking to a group of Year 2s the teacher asked each child individually during circle time what they wanted to achieve over the next few weeks. One said to make more friends and other children, when asked, said they would like to help her in making new friends. There then shot up a group of very eager young children wishing to be her friend.

All these things will help those participating to learn about each other, and the more we understand and know about each other the more we develop a sense of belonging to the group, as the other members also know and understand you. Within the classroom, as you build acceptance and the students experience this, they are more likely to be supportive to others. This will lead on to being more supportive and helpful, more considerate of others and more accepting of others, including those now in their friendship group.

This enquiry time will also provide you with the opportunity to find out what is important to them individually. Remember that making things relevant is the most important of the 3 M's, so when a specific young person comes across a problem or difficulty, look at what they are wanting to achieve personally over the next year and see how the motivation to achieve it can be channelled through the problem they are facing. Character and resilience are built through life's problems and they can be developed when working towards a specific personal aim.

Speak to the group as a whole and get them to appreciate that you see every one of them as important and valued.

You have the influence to impact upon a child's sense of belonging by the way you single them out. If you consistently highlight the poor behaviour of one child or a group of children over others, they will inevitably feel less and less part of the 'good' group and this in turn can work towards them not feeling part of your class. So, when needing to have a word about something which needs correcting, do your best to do so privately or at least back up your comments later with some positive comments again for the whole class to hear.

If on the other hand you constantly praise and commend one child over another, you will be showing to the rest of the group you have a favourite. This can work positively as it might mean they have, as a consequence of this, more friends because of your attention, or it could mean that you start to divide the class between those who agree with you and like the person and those who feel left out.

This approach requires a constant evaluation of how the students are beginning to work together as a group. But just as a socially responsible company monitors the mental well-being of staff, so you should also monitor the mental well-being of your class and build upon a sense of belonging for all. These things which have been highlighted are part of the way we as humans monitor our position within groups. It can be said to apply to the way adults think as well; it's just that as young people they are ill-equipped emotionally to deal with the implications of group dynamics. Findings show that classroom peer status has more impact than friendship on significantly predicting school perceptions, school involvement and performance. Rejected children have significantly less favourable perceptions of school, higher levels of school avoidance, and lower levels of school performance than popular, average or neglected children within the classroom (Wentzel and Asher, 1995).

Bear in mind that the young people you teach may be going through lots of issues outside of school which might be affecting and impacting on their sense of belonging. If their situation is poor outside of school, they may bring their frustrations into school. Often those who suffer rejections demonstrate their feelings of rejection through poor behaviour and often anger. This poor behaviour and anger are the very things that make it hard for that person to find a sense of belonging, gain friends and be liked in the first place.

Do your utmost to recognise that sometimes those who have the poorest behaviour have the greatest need to find a sense of belonging somewhere. If they get to the stage of having to be removed from your class because of the effect of their behaviour on others, then do try to get to know that person outside the lesson and share with them what you are doing within the class, and how others are doing, so they still feel that they are valued and included by you. Remember that the feeling of any emotion stirs the related urge to act. Young people feeling rejected will act out with frustration and anger. Feeling included and supported will help them respond more positively to maintain that good feeling.

Critical questions

»   *What actions do you take which help young people to feel included and have a sense of belonging within your class?*

»   *What do you do/say in the opening few seconds every time you see the children at the start of the lesson?*

»   *Do you have favourites, and do you think the class knows this?*

»   *Is your favouritism linked to their educational ability?*

»   *How do you reaffirm the sense of belonging throughout your time with the class?*

»   *Do you have students you find difficult to handle and do you think the rest of the class knows this?*

»   *Does this also have a correlation with their ability to perform academically?*

»   *What can you do to get to know the person who perhaps doesn't feel they belong?*

»   *How can you get to know what each person you teach values and wants to achieve with you?*

»   *How do you build supportive interaction within your class?*

Autonomy

Ryan (1995; Ryan and Belmont, 1991; Ryan and Lynch, 1989) has suggested that autonomy develops most effectively in situations where children and teenagers feel a sense of belonging, as discussed earlier. This is an important point because it challenges an assumption that fostering independence among adolescents requires a reduction in personal closeness.

According to Ryan (1995), it is important to remember that autonomy does not mean detachment from others; instead, it refers to the individual's sense of agency or self-determination in a social context. Students and young people who experience autonomy will perceive themselves to have choice and will also experience a connection between their actions and personal goals (Connell and Wellborn, 1991).

This is another very good reason to find out what motivates each person you are seeking to teach and educate. No matter how young they are, explore with them what they are wanting to achieve.

Classroom climate

Deci et al (1981) used an instrument to assess teachers' styles, reasoning that some teachers are oriented towards supporting students' autonomy whereas others are oriented towards controlling students' behaviour.

It has been clearly shown that the teacher's behaviour – the degree to which they use either a controlling or autonomy supportive approach – has an important effect on students' motivation and self-determination. In their research, students and young people who were autonomy-supportive were more intrinsically motivated and had a higher perception of their cognitive competence and self-worth than did those students in classrooms with controlling teachers (Deci et al, 1981).

This can be especially hard on young people as they experience the need for more autonomy throughout their adolescence, whereas in fact opportunity for autonomy within the classroom decreases as they enter secondary education.

So how do we provide a classroom that helps motivate students and young people to be more intrinsically motivated? You have to bear in mind that in order to do this you will be requiring them to use and develop their executive function of their brain, and as we have seen the brain is under development during their time at school. It will also require you to be instructive and guiding and, in some instances, gently controlling through their early years but always looking out for the time when you can encourage autonomy.

Research has shown that autonomy improves self-regulation because it fosters openness to failures (Koestner and Zuckerman, 1994; Hodgins and Liebeskind, 2003; Weinstein et al, 2011).

Phrases such as *'you can try'*, *'you might'*, *'if you choose'* and *'we ask you to'* are statements that encourage the listener to engage and reflect, and seek out their own way to do something.

When meeting a new group I always start by finding out what technique I should use when I need the whole class to listen.

CASE STUDY

I was asked to deliver a whole-day workshop highlighting the significant brain development and changes that 14–15-year-olds will experience to 120 Year 9 students in a hall. You can imagine how it was at the start of the day, trying to get them all to be quiet for someone they had never met before. The headteacher took charge and they became quiet as he raised his voice over the noise and I was introduced. I did a quick introduction to what would be happening during the day and who I was before going on to ask them the question, 'How would you like me to gain quiet?' I explained that normally when dealing with adults I just raise my hand, and ask if they thought that would be acceptable for them. They agreed, and this was put to the test after lunch when no teacher had yet returned to the hall, yet the vast majority of students had.

The noise level, as you can imagine, was high but this time by raising my hand within 15 seconds I had the hall quiet and was able to talk to them all as the teachers came in to silence.

Method

One method you could try within the classroom to develop autonomy deals with the issue of getting students and young people to hand in their homework on time. This is a good organisational skill for them to learn and their time in school is a good place to learn it.

Ask them how they could make sure that you as a teacher can have confidence that they will all remember to hand in their homework on time. Explore methods that they think they could adopt and let them develop their skills to accomplish it. See if group responsibility might help. Buddy systems, where they remind each other with texts, might also be useful. Offer ideas but let them know that the problem is theirs to learn to manage.

Another area of autonomy you might tackle is how they wish to learn a specific subject. Would they like to work individually or within groups? Would they like a textbook or for lessons to be more teacher-led or discursive? Co-operative learning is significant for the development of peer relations; it also directly affects the students' interaction, and the nature of that interaction, if implemented in a positive manner.

When you experience an issue with a student or young person, recognise that it is just as much their issue as it is yours or those that are affected by it. We often find ways of telling a young person what they should do rather than providing them with the opportunity to tell us what it is they can do or could try to do. Help them take ownership of their lives and then find the best way to manage the issue together.

Critical questions

» *How can you start to provide opportunity within your classroom for autonomy?*

» *Do you provide more autonomy to those who are more academically able?*

» *In which areas of learning can you develop their autonomy?*

» *What three things relating to their emotional development would you like students to take more responsibility for?*

Self-esteem (social and emotional competence)

The third area we should consider relating to the caring and supporting of young people is in the area of their own self-esteem, which is born out of their own social and emotional competence.

Building a community

In effect, what you are trying to build within your classroom and school is a community where each member can feel that the group will satisfy their needs, they will feel supported and cared for, and that they will feel valued and their contribution to the group will be respected. Put quite simply, each member needs to feel they belong. You can become not only an educator of your subject but a facilitator of each young person's personal journey towards adulthood.

It may sound a tall order, but I believe that the biggest fundamental change needed within the educational system is that we should make schools into better communities of caring. This can start with what you aim to do within your classroom, which is often seen in a variety of different ways by those who attend. It could be a place of excitement, or fear; a place of discovery or a place of dread. It could be a place to find acceptance, or a place of isolation; a place of friends and support, or a place of insult and ridicule. In short, your classroom can become a place where young people's self-esteem can be built up or knocked down, and the measure of what happens in there can determine their own social and emotional competence and ability to participate meaningfully within the school as well as the adult world.

Building self-worth

The first two aspects of providing a safe BASE go a long way to providing what is needed for young people to be engaged, improving motivation and learning. These opportunities need to also be linked to the person's own ability to make mistakes but feel safe to do so, and also the knowledge that if they are having difficulty they are surrounded by others who will offer support. There is a lot of research to suggest that problems with self-esteem and anxiety in young people are increasing. Self-doubt is not just restricted to young people. I have many conversations with adults which reflect the anxiety they feel about their own inadequacy at times. It seems to be part of who we are to examine and judge ourselves against others. Too often, those we choose to judge ourselves against do not provide a true comparison to us; this therefore leads to those feelings of inadequacy.

What you need to do as an educator is work with the people who come under your influence and be determined to help them build up a true understanding of their own competence, self-worth and ability. You need to help them to recognise what it is they are able to achieve for themselves as a social human being first and foremost, and then show them how to use their own ability and confidence to do their best when it comes to their education as well.

Too often, I hear throwaway comments from teachers who expect high levels of compliance from those they seek to teach, especially at a young age when children are more emotionally sensitive. Comments such as:

> 'If you don't do it properly then you will lose your break.'

> 'If the boys want to get it wrong and be bad then that's up to them, you girls don't have to copy them.'

> 'You know what you should be doing, get on with it.'

> 'How many times have I told you?'

> 'Yes you can do it, just get on with it.'

When I talk with young people who have been spoken to by a teacher regarding their behaviour within the classroom, they often tell me that the teacher hates them. This is a very long way from what the teacher actually feels, which is more along the lines of, *'I don't hate them; it's what they do I don't like.'*

So, where has the problem arisen? Consider what is going on within a young person's mind when they are being told off. First and foremost, they see that those who are telling them off are often annoyed with them. The person doing the telling off may have inadvertently shown frustration towards them and told them what has caused their frustration. This feeling will inevitably cause a reaction within the child, and they will be triggered emotionally to how they are being spoken to. They may be thinking or feeling any or all of the following.

- They may be thinking about others who are also hearing what is being said to them.

- They might be reminded of other occasions when they have been spoken to like this and what they did or felt as a consequence on those previous occasions.

- They will be thinking about what is being said to them and usually find a way to rebut what is being said in order to defend themselves.

- They may well look for others to blame or point the finger at, or think of a reason why they did what they did.

All these responses are a self-evaluation of themselves and how they feel about the situation. As a consequence, they will look towards finding an ending to the 'teacher talk' that is as self-protecting as it can be. This could cover a multitude of responses, for example saying sorry, saying nothing or even trying to ignore the issue and move on. Whatever is going through the young person's mind, you as the person speaking to them will be affecting their own self-esteem and their sense of belonging. If these two things are not taken into account during or after the conversation, then the person's self-esteem will be affected and this will often cause the young person to go and seek comfort with others and complain about how they have felt in a negative way regarding you, or to release some frustration later in the day on how they have been made to feel.

Any conversation with another person affects the other person's view of you and also of themselves. As educators and teachers of young people, we often want them when being corrected or reprimanded to reflect upon what is being said and to make better choices in light of what has been said the next time such a situation occurs. While it is very noble of us to think or hope that, it is often a totally unrealistic situation considering the level of emotional ability, emotional intelligence and often the mental faculty that we know young people have who are just starting on their journey towards brain maturation and social competence. Young people need to learn these skills, and we should not assume they already have them and have chosen not to use them. It is like me overhearing once an adult talking to her dog and saying frustratedly, 'Eat properly!', as the dog gobbled down the food put in front of her!

Young people's self-esteem is always being challenged within the classroom as we are constantly attempting to challenge them to learn, often in situations they find stressful and towards things they find irrelevant, without taking into account the myriad of other events which are impacting upon their young lives. The least we can do when they do something that is inconsistent with how they should be behaving, socially and emotionally, is to use that time to support them and let them know that they still belong, are valued, and that we can help and support them as they explore better choices with their actions.

This might require us taking time to talk to them after the initial talk to reaffirm with them, but it needs to be done as the way we impact on them will mean the difference between them being able to engage with us educationally and socially or not. The last comment I always say to a child when they are pushing or acting in a frustrating manner and I have had to intervene as their behaviour was going beyond their own ability to rein it in, is something appropriately affirming for them as well as to let them know they are still valued by me. I often conclude the conversation using the same firm tone to show the depth of my belief with these words:

> *The reason we are having this conversation and I have taken the time to talk with you is because I think you are one of the best students I teach and I know you are a lot better than the behaviour that I have just seen.*

If you think that they perhaps haven't reached the heights of being one of your best students then you can say. *'You have the potential to be one of the best...'* Also make sure you have something that reminds them of something good that you have seen them do, which shows in strict contrast the behaviour they are now showing.

It's important to keep the tone stern as you don't want to bring any confusion into the telling off, rather to emphasise that the whole process is serious. Always ask as well what they think about what you have said. You need feedback and you are also seeking for them to reflect upon their actions but more importantly on the things you have said.

They must go away from a situation that has been bad recognising that it was bad and that it should not happen again. They also need to understand that the reason they don't want it to happen again is because they are better than that particular piece of bad behaviour.

Fostering compliance does not mean that young people learn to become socially competent; they simply learn to be compliant. A study carried out with parents who adopted high levels of compliance without taking into account the needs of the child showed that this can result in children having low social competence, low self-esteem and aggressiveness (Battistich et al, 1991, 1995).

These issues and types of poor behaviour very often result in young people being taken out of class and given alternative lessons, which simply compounds the problems of low self-esteem and aggressiveness. Teachers in primary schools have a wonderful opportunity to help teach social and emotional competences to young people, as long as they take into account the needs of the child to have that sense of belonging and autonomy and they look to protect the young person's self-esteem, providing the BASE that is needed.

CASE STUDY

Topcliffe Primary School, Birmingham

Topcliffe Primary is primarily a one-form entry school in Castle Vale, Birmingham; however, it also has one of the largest resource bases for children who have autism or speech and language difficulties. Currently, Castle Vale is in the lowest 10 per cent for social deprivation and unemployment across the country. Consequently, for a large proportion of families in Castle Vale, poor mental health, low self-esteem and confidence are huge factors. Due to the increased expectations on children within education, mental health is also becoming a major factor within schools. Therefore, as a school, it was decided that something must be done.

At the beginning of the academic year, Topcliffe began working closely alongside Victor to create a bespoke programme that could support our children. It was decided that the focus would be to support the children at Topcliffe and to raise their aspirations, confidence and self-belief. Together, we looked at the current Building Mental Security programme and began to adapt it to not only be suitable for a primary school, but also be suitable for our children with a diagnosis of AS.

This year, we introduced Building Mental Security across our whole school including our resource bases. Each teacher has received training on how to deliver the programme. This was then monitored and reviewed to see how certain sessions have been delivered and adapted to suit the needs of the learners.

At Topcliffe, it is expected that every class is to deliver a 20-minute session linked to the BMS value for that week. This value should be discussed throughout the week to help children to contextualise its meaning. In addition, a 'shared folder' on our school curriculum has been created where staff can regularly share any resources created for the session.

From observations and feedback from the teachers, it is clear to see that children enjoy learning about themselves and others in their classroom and many of the sessions provide opportunities for this to happen. Through circle times and class discussions, children are benefitting from an exposure of these in-depth, quality conversations. This has meant that children have the opportunity to voice their opinion and increase their understanding about these sensitive and sometimes never-before-discussed subjects.

The impact of the Building Mental Security programme is difficult to assess due to the nature of the issues it addresses. However, already more positive peer-to-peer relationships have been forming within school as well as a greater awareness of other children and their differences. Also, the teachers' viewpoint on mental health has improved, with many of the teachers now thinking more about the children's well-being and happiness. We will be continuing to work with Victor in the future to help us to embed these key values into our school ethos.

Critical questions

» *How do your comments when dealing with problems help maintain a person's self-esteem?*

» *Do you ever use comments that highlight your frustration?*

» *Do your instructions focus upon compliance or on autonomy?*

» *How can you encourage autonomy and also raise or maintain self-esteem?*

Chapter reflections

This chapter has looked at the three basic psychological needs for human growth and development, which are belonging, autonomy and self-esteem (competence): BASE.

» *The sense of belonging underpins who we are and how we are able to cope with the situations in which we find ourselves.*

» *Building a sense of belonging within the classroom and school helps in the motivation and engagement of young people. We as educators and teachers need to create a classroom that everyone feels they belong to, where they can share and feel valued and even when they do something wrong they can learn through the situation, knowing that the relationship has still been maintained.*

» *We looked at how to improve autonomy within lessons so that young people and students learn to take control of their actions and their lives.*

» *Your leadership and influence will be an example to those you seek to teach, and you are teaching more than just a lesson; you are demonstrating social and emotional competences that you wish them to mirror.*

Taking it further

Take time to get to know your students and provide them time for getting to know one another. Look to see what aspects of their learning they can take responsibility for. Provide them with the time to decide when they bring in their homework as long as it fits into your timetable as well. Help them to develop social responsibility for their own learning. The more you develop that and the less you aim to get them to just be compliant, the more motivated and engaged they will feel.

References

Battistich, V, Watson, M, Solomon, D, Schaps, E and Solomon, J (1991) The Child Development Project: A Comprehensive Program for the Development of Prosocial Character. In Kurtines, W M and Gerwirtz, J L (eds) *Handbook of Moral Behavior and Development, Vol. 1. Theory; Vol. 2. Research; Vol. 3. Application* (pp 1–34). Hillsdale, NJ: Lawrence Erlbaum Associates, Inc.

Battistich, V, Solomon, D, Dong-il, K, Watson, M and Schaps, E (1995) Schools as Communities, Poverty Levels of Student Populations, and Students' Attitudes, Motives, and Performance: A Multilevel Analysis. *American Educational Research Journal*, 32(3): 627–58.

Connell, J and Wellborn, J (1991) Competence, Autonomy, and Relatedness: A Motivational Analysis of Self-System Processes. *Journal of Personality and Social Psychology*, 65.

Deci, E L, Schwartz, A J, Sheinman, L and Ryan, R M (1981) An Instrument to Assess Adults' Orientations Toward Control Versus Autonomy with Children: Reflections on Intrinsic Motivation and Perceived Competence. *Journal of Educational Psychology*, 73(5): 642–50.

Deci, E L, Valleyrand, R J, Pelletier, L and Ryan, R M (1991) Motivation and Education: The Self-Determination Perspective. *Educational Psychologist*, 26, 352–46.

Hodgins, H S and Liebeskind, E (2003) Apology Versus Defense: Antecedents and Consequences. *Journal of Experimental Social Psychology*, 39: 297–36.

Koestner, R and Zuckerman, M (1994) Causality Orientations, Failure, and Achievement. *Journal of Personality*, 62(3): 321–46.

Ryan, R M (1995) Psychological Needs and the Facilitation of Integrative Processes. *Journal of Psychology*, 63(3): 397–427.

Ryan, R M and Belmont, M (1991*) Autonomy and Relatedness as Fundamental Motives in Learning and Development*. Paper presented at the annual conference of the American Educational Research Association, Chicago.

Ryan, R M and Lynch, J (1989) Emotional Autonomy Versus Detachment: Revisiting the Vicissitudes of Adolescence and Young Adulthood. *Child Development*, 60: 340–56.

Weinstein, M, Ben-Sira, L, Levy, Y, Zachor, D A, Ben Itzhak, E, Artzi, M, Tarrasch, R, Eksteine, P M, Hendler, T and Ben Bashat, D (2011) Abnormal White Matter Integrity in Young Children with Autism. *Human Brain Mapping*, 32(4): 534–43.

Wentzel, K R and Asher, S R (1995) The Academic Lives of Neglected, Rejected, Popular, and Controversial Children. *Child Development*, 66(3): 754–63.

6 Emotionally intelligent relationships

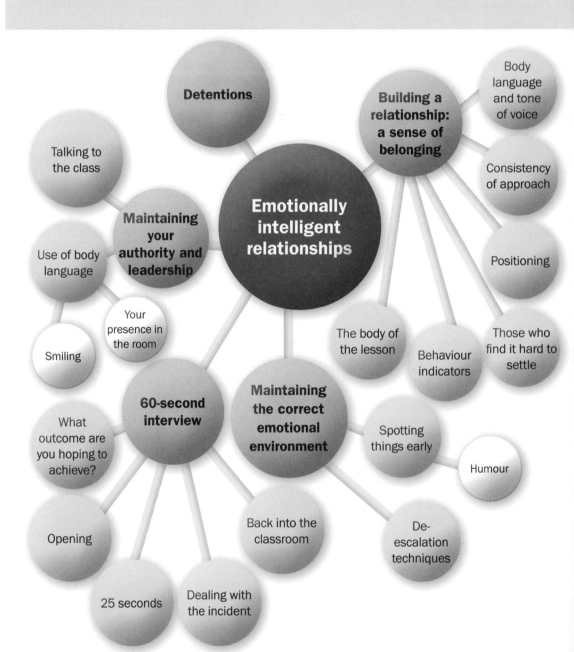

Emotionally intelligent relationships

- Detentions
- Building a relationship: a sense of belonging
  - Body language and tone of voice
  - Consistency of approach
  - Positioning
  - Those who find it hard to settle
  - Behaviour indicators
- Talking to the class
- Maintaining your authority and leadership
  - Use of body language
  - Smiling
  - Your presence in the room
- The body of the lesson
- Maintaining the correct emotional environment
  - Spotting things early
  - Humour
  - De-escalation techniques
  - Back into the classroom
- 60-second interview
  - What outcome are you hoping to achieve?
  - Opening
  - 25 seconds
  - Dealing with the incident

Knowing that we can control our own behaviour makes it more likely that we will.
Peter Singer (www.brainyquote.com/quotes/quotes/p/petersinge471270.html)

Introduction

Over the coming years of your teaching career you will find yourself building up a catalogue of skills, not only on how to teach your lessons but also on how to manage your classroom. I hope the first four chapters have helped you to lay a foundation on which to build your emotional skills, to understand what you see in front of you but also the possible reasons as to why those things are occurring.

Over the next few chapters, I will discuss practical tools for interaction with your students, to help to preserve and encourage good behaviour. I will also look at methods that can help to de-escalate difficult situations.

All behaviour is an outcome of a number of factors, some of which you can control, others in which you will only be a bystander. Your aim is to control the one thing that you can: yourself. From managing yourself you can help the students manage themselves. They need to learn, as we all do, to own what they are doing and not, as is often the case, to try to excuse their behaviour as the result of others' actions.

When your young children and students are with you in your classroom, they are subconsciously trying to manage their thoughts and feelings in the context of what is going on around them. We must appreciate and understand that their ability to do this isn't fully developed, but we also mustn't excuse it as being out of their control. They may not yet have mastered their thoughts and emotions but, with our help and guidance, they can be developing the skills to do so. That is what we are offering to them when they start to lose control or get carried away by situations. We offer guidance and solutions to improve and make appropriate choices rather than punishment and blame for their lack of skills.

Detentions

I don't have an issue with giving detentions or detaching a student from a lesson or situation if their behaviour has made it inappropriate for them to remain within the class. However, detentions need to be used to reflect on what went wrong and work together to seek solutions in order to avoid a recurrence. To have a student or young child detained at their inconvenience, without any input from an adult who understands and can talk them through the areas in which they need to improve and manage their behaviour, and expect them to grasp the necessary skills to do better next time in order to avoid a punishment is not, I believe, the most efficient use of time or a recipe for building a relationship with them.

If a student does the same thing wrong twice or especially three times and the only consequence for the student over this time is that the punishments get harsher, without any change in behaviour, this should highlight a need for a different approach. Including parents, or requiring the student to sign an improvement contract often misses the point that the student may want to change but he/she hasn't been shown how to manage the emotional impulses triggered by the attitude and situations that he/she faces within school.

Building a relationship: a sense of belonging

The art of being a good teacher is being able to build good, strong, respectful relationships with your students. Your involvement can be key to making the difference, and it is also one of the greatest joys, as you watch your students travel through the different stages of their lives. You have to create an environment of safety and trust on which to build knowledge for life as well as for the academic subject. To do this, you need to watch how events in the classroom are affecting the students' emotions and identify areas of development, both emotionally and academically. Any area of classroom interaction can involve the emotional part of the brain taking over in a good or negative way, and we need to watch and manage that as best we can. Introducing games or competitions will engage the emotional part of the brain as fun is being introduced, but this will need to be controlled so that it doesn't get over-excited and move into silliness. So the thinking part of the brain needs to be encouraged to manage the fun in a sensible way.

As discussed in earlier chapters, the 'emotional' brain develops faster than the 'thinking' part of the brain, and so it is ready to kick in almost instantaneously when triggered by any provocation. We have to be able to manage our tone and language in order to keep the thinking brain engaged and manage the emotional brain. If we can see that emotions are taking over, we must act in a way that gives the student a chance to re-engage their thinking brain and start to manage their emotions, by de-escalating the situation or deflecting their attention.

Before any task that may involve the students moving away from the normal classroom activity, for example practical lessons in science, the tendency is to tell the students what we don't want them to do or to warn them that any silliness will result in the activity being stopped. Here I suggest that you explain beforehand what you are going be doing and then ask them what kinds of behaviour you will be expecting from them. What will they have to look out for? And also ask who will find staying sensible tricky? You can do this by letting them know that you appreciate that it may be hard for them to stay on task, but you will be helping them and may require them to step outside to refocus before returning for the activity. The aim is to look after and coach those you know are going to find it tricky, rather than start with being hard on them with threats of punishment. If they fail, then it has more to do with their ability to focus, and remember that is very rarely improved with punishment.

Body language and tone of voice

When observing NQTs, one of the most common things on which I give feedback is the use of their body language and tone of voice. Both of these things are affected when we are under stress and both need to be managed and overcome to enable us to demonstrate control and authority.

Maintaining control of a classroom involves constant vigilance – your positioning and tone of voice within the classroom can have a calming effect upon the class just as easily as it can create an environment for misbehaviour and silliness.

Consistency of approach

Consistency and familiarity are important for building a relationship with a class. Each school will have its own set of ground rules that teachers should follow – these build familiarity and allow both staff and pupils to understand expectations of behaviour. Some schools will expect pupils to line up outside the room. In others, students will be expected to enter the class quietly and stand behind chairs. Whatever you are guided to do, it is very important for you to be consistent in doing it. The more consistent you are, the more quickly you will gain control of the classroom. Swapping and changing things to see what works best will only cause confusion, and this in turn will encourage behavioural problems.

Positioning

Have one set position within the classroom from which you always start the lesson. This should be where all students can have easy eye contact with you. You need to be standing as this will give the element of control. This starting position will help students get used to focusing on you to be ready to receive the first instructions.

Speak with calmness, expectation, hope and encouragement and, if possible, have a smile on your face, as this will add to the feeling of calmness and build upon the warm greeting you gave them at the door. It will also keep you focused upon how you are feeling.

Those who find it hard to settle

Students will sometimes find it hard to settle for a number of reasons – perhaps they're just back from an exciting lunch break or have been having a laugh with friends on the way to the classroom. This is a guidance and encouragement opportunity with which to start, not a discipline issue.

There are a number of ways to deal with this.

- Move towards where the students are seated while talking to other students along the way, commenting on good things that others are doing or have done within your class or with their homework. You can also make comments about good social behaviour.

- Try to gain eye contact with the offending students and see if a frown or just a look will have the desired effect. There is a difference between making eye contact and maintaining eye contact; three seconds is optimal for maintaining eye contact, but don't get drawn into a staring contest. It is just meant as a statement for them to engage with you. If they do, then a nod of approval and a smile to affirm your pleasure towards them is sufficient to keep a good relationship. If not, then continue to move towards them, casually giving them the chance to amend their ways by choice.

- Once you have arrived near their desks, your presence will add to the reason to stop messing around and start to get control of themselves a little better. Ask them a question such as *'Are you OK for the start of the lesson?'* Your tone should be one of calmness and with no hint of annoyance – just very plain and ordinary. The mention of 'lesson' along with the question regarding how they are and the tone will all help them to engage their thinking brain and take control. The first to start to focus should be thanked, followed by a comment such as *'It's good to have you here. Let's hope we have a good lesson as I think you will do well in this.'*

You will notice that we are not telling them to behave, what they should do or what you want them to do. All those things are obvious and they know them. All you are interested in doing is helping them start to control themselves now that the lesson has begun. You are also giving them an opportunity to work together to calm down, and you will see who is the leader and follower within the group. This will be useful if you have to talk to them again.

Peer pressure and acceptance are very important in teenage years, and copying each other is a very good bonding experience for them. One person on their own messing about is very rare and often a sign of other issues. A group messing about is typical and also self-motivating, so when the leader of the group starts to calm down the others tend to follow. You should be able to spot the 'ring leaders' in any class, although they might not see themselves as such, and it is good to work with them to develop good social skills.

The behaviour is not to be seen as 'bad'. It is just inappropriate and so should be tackled as such. Once they are calm, and later in the lesson, you can talk to them about their start and ask them how they think they could do it better the next time – what things could they do to help calm themselves down so that you can start the lesson more quickly?

Behaviour indicators

Inappropriate behaviour may be linked to high spirits but it may also be an avoidance technique so as not to have to start the lesson. How many times have you done things simply to avoid having to do something that you don't want to do? Try to develop skills in looking for the reasons for a chosen behaviour rather than categorising people negatively. Low confidence, feelings of inadequacy or lack of sleep could all be contributing factors and therefore should be taken into consideration when dealing with poor behaviour. If you don't, then the poor behaviour will keep recurring. I will discuss in a later chapter some of the problems that you might encounter in relation to special needs, and sometimes students can go under the radar because the teacher's focus has been diverted towards more obvious issues. Don't assume that every child has been assessed and everything is known about them. You may be the first one to notice something and it won't hurt to see if others have noticed anything different or looked at other possible reasons for a child's behaviour.

The body of the lesson

An engaging start is important and is also a good time to, if possible, bring in elements of the spiritual, moral, social and cultural development (SMSC) of pupils. This is looked for within lessons and forms part of Ofsted's criteria for outstanding lessons. The importance of making it relevant must be remembered and people are usually very happy to talk about their own experiences and opinions. Helping students to challenge their own preconceived ideas about a topic is a good starting point.

The important thing is to get the lesson correctly differentiated, engaging and relevant, with clear learning outcomes and measurable targets for students to be working towards. The more you concentrate on these points, the fewer problems you will have within your lesson.

You will notice very quickly if you are not meeting those criteria as the attention of the class will easily get drawn away from you and the subject, as discussed in Chapter 4.

Critical questions

»   *How much do you consider that the clothes you wear affect your students?*

»   *How important to you is where you stand and start the lesson?*

»   *Do you think that you have a set method for moving around the class, perhaps avoiding some students or spending too long with others? Is this influenced more by a few poorly behaved students than you considering the needs of the whole class?*

»   *Have you got into lazy habits such as sitting at your desk and having the students come to you, or sitting on the edge of tables?*

»   *How do you use your tone to affect the classroom?*

»   *Do you use a calm voice to achieve calm or a loud shouting voice to achieve calm?*

»   *Think back over your last difficult lesson. Try to remember the kind of tone you were using. Was it being influenced by your emotions and the situation in the classroom?*

Maintaining your authority and leadership

Talking to the class

Consider your body language at all times and watch to see that you maintain movement with your eyes as well as your body. What I mean is, don't just focus on one or two students who are looking at you and paying attention, and don't stand stock still when talking with the whole class. Both are signs of nerves and will be picked up by the class. Remember that you inspire confidence by your body language and tone of voice.

Use of body language

Smiling

Remember to smile as often as you can when it is appropriate and fitting with the situation. I am saddened to hear that new teachers are still told *not to smile until Christmas*. Please do, and please make your classroom a place of smiles. I can only assume that perhaps whoever is giving these instructions means *don't be overtly friendly*, and that is a good warning, but not smiling at your students for four months is just going too far. Here are a few positive aspects of smiling and I hope that it becomes part of your life, not just in the classroom.

- Smiling is contagious.

  The complex brain activity that occurs when you see someone smiling means that smiles spread. Studies report that just seeing one person smiling activates the area of your brain that controls your facial movement, which leads to a grin. Even in bad situations, if you smile, others are likely to mimic the expression (Gutman, 2011).

- You'll decrease stress and anxiety.

  It's not easy to keep smiling in stressful situations, but studies report that doing exactly that has health benefits. When recovering from a stressful situation, study participants who were smiling had lower heart rates than those with a neutral facial expression. So, the next time you're feeling stressed, just try smiling to calm yourself down (Helpguide.org, 2014).

- Smiling releases endorphins.

  Smiling decreases stress and anxiety by releasing endorphins, chemicals that make you happier. Endorphins are the same chemicals you get from working out or running, resulting in what is known as a runner's high.

- You'll be more approachable.

  A smile suggests that you're personable, easy going and empathetic.

- Smiling strengthens your immune system.

  Smiling even makes your immune system stronger by making your body produce white blood cells to help fight illness. One study found that hospitalised children who were visited by story-tellers and puppeteers who made them smile and laugh had higher white blood cell counts than those children who weren't visited (Béres and Major, 2011).

- You'll be friendlier.

  Studies have found that people are more willing to engage socially with others who are smiling. A smile is an inviting facial expression that tells people you are willing to talk and interact with them (Gutman, 2011).

- Smiling will make you more comfortable.

  Our natural tendency is to stick to things that are familiar, but smiling decreases this need. A study found that smiling can make you more comfortable in situations where you would otherwise feel awkward (Gutman, 2011).

- You'll seem more trustworthy.

  Trusting doesn't come easily to many, but smiling at someone may help. Participants in a University of Pittsburgh study rated people who smiled as more trustworthy than people with non-smiling facial expressions (Schmidt et al, 2012). So, if you want to improve your credibility, simply smile more. What could be easier than that?

- You'll be a better leader.

  Smiling is a more effective leadership technique than having great management responsibilities. When used appropriately, it shows connection and confidence.

So, the next time you really want to show off those leadership skills, just smile!

I think that has given enough reasons to make smiling a part of your lessons straight away and not to hold back on those benefits for four months.

Your presence in the room

Along with your smile will go your actual presence within the room. Your body language and how you hold yourself will communicate a vast amount of information to those that you meet. Here are a few tips that will raise the confidence, credibility and authority you portray, along with a few things to watch out for.

- When you want students to listen to you, keep yourself level, especially your head. Stand as straight as you can and make your head level and then just move your head as if it is a periscope on a submarine and you are scanning the sea. Keep your body still, as stillness is an authoritative behaviour, and try not to move your shoulders as you move your head.

- When talking, keep any gestures in the gesture box. Your gestures alone reveal your confidence or lack of it. The most effective movements take place within the gesture box, which is no higher than your sternum and no lower than your hips and no wider than your shoulders. The 'sweet spot' is your navel as this is where gestures appear the most natural. When you start talking and want to appear relaxed and in control, get your hands involved immediately, you will link with your students through interactive gestures, so if your mouth is moving then so should your hands be.

- Eye contact. When talking, try speaking one phrase as you scan the room, resting and making eye contact for one or two seconds with those who are listening and three seconds with those who are struggling. Again, once you see that they are back on track you can nod your head as approval to them and they will get the message.

- Listen actively. Your credibility can be won and lost through your listening. Tune your ears to what you are being asked as well as any little comments that someone makes, as those comments may carry a lot of insight and definitely carry a train of thought from the speaker. This will help you identify the direction in which the ideas and lesson are going. If a student has asked you a question, a slight raising of the head helps with focus and pointing your body towards them provides a sense of attention. Pay attention to what others are doing at the same time as listening, using peripheral vision to pick up on body language and movement. Use your palms outstretched in a stop movement towards anyone who you want to stop what they are doing, without looking away from the one doing right. People's needs when it comes to being listened to include being valued, appreciated, understood, respected and comfortable that they can share with you. If any one of these is missing it will reduce the effectiveness of your own communication with them.

- Avoid speech fillers. I am sure that at times you have been more interested in counting how often during a talk someone says, *you know, like* or *er.* I did find myself saying the word *'OK'* until someone kindly pointed out to me that I had started to reach the twenties. It was a good time for me to well, you know, to like, er, well, start to er, look at, well, you know, fillers, like OK. See, I only say it once now!

- Avoid over-correcting yourself. It is easy when you are feeling self-conscious to overreact to your every mistake, if you trip over a word or the laptop isn't working, or you haven't managed to get round to everyone. When mistakes happen, simply correct them and move on. They don't require comments; it will only highlight your preoccupation with internally criticising yourself.

- Avoid masking your face and hands. This tends to creep up on you when you begin to feel uneasy. It takes many forms and may include crossing your arms or hugging yourself, pulling your feet and legs closer together, playing with your clothes or jewellery. In men, it often encourages the stroking of the chin and throat or holding your hands in front of your mouth. Stroking your throat can also be a sign of nervousness and is often accompanied with squeezing your throat and chin between the thumb and fingers slightly. It's a form of hiding and comforting yourself, not really what you want to be demonstrating in front of students you are meant to be leading.

The point of all this is to get you used to monitoring yourself, watching for clues that signal how you are feeling and making sure that at all times you demonstrate a sense of confidence and authority. Shouting and raising your voice can often provide the exact opposite of what is intended if the corresponding body language doesn't match the tone. Try to record yourself to see how you are coming across. I was interested to note that David Cameron practised not only his body language while delivering a speech but also how he was going to walk to the stage during his party conference, so that he got it right. He understands that it isn't just the words he is delivering that are important, it is from the very moment he is seen by people that they will be registering what they think of him and whether he meets their hopes and expectations.

Maintaining the correct emotional environment

It is your responsibility to maintain the correct emotional atmosphere within the classroom, but to do this with a diverse mix of students who really only have their age in common is a challenge. Yet for that hour or so, you have keep them calm, focused and productive. The most effective method is to spot things early and to see what you can do to either de-escalate situations or to deflect attention in a new direction.

Spotting things early

The greeting at the door is a time for you to be checking body language, eye contact and general demeanour, as all will let you know what frame of mind students are coming into your lesson in. Some of you will find it easier than others to read the emotional messages people give out, but it is a skill that you need to hone as it will help nip things in the bud.

Young people are practising their emotions and therefore will often dramatise and over-demonstrate a specific feeling, which will help you, but get used to noticing differences in demeanour so you can ask students early what is going on or if there's anything wrong. If you don't pick up on the signs then students will often behave in a way that forces you to react. This is known as attention seeking and quite rightly so, as students are trying to get direction, help, support, comfort, recognition; the list goes on, but basically they want to have some acknowledgment regarding who they are and what they are feeling. This is not to be seen as negative, rather it is inappropriate attention seeking. As a guide and educator, your task is to help students move towards correct attention-seeking behaviour, by being on task and fulfilling what is being asked of them rather than distracting others or avoiding the task.

If you notice that a student is not happy or that they are too happy, then at some point you will need to help get them focused upon the lesson, either by enquiring what is wrong or by helping them to control their behaviour. This is to be done early and quickly and should not have to draw you away from the body of the class – it is purely aimed at letting the student know that something isn't right and that you have noticed. This will help to stop them from becoming even more demonstrative and obvious. It will also demonstrate that you are sensitive and caring, which others will notice. As mentioned earlier, your students are very interested in peer influences and watching what their friends and others are doing. They will also be learning from and watching adults, and especially copying adults who they like or who have an influence on their lives.

Remember that what you are doing with your interactions with one person is often being assessed by 29 others, so make sure that how you deal with them is also a physical demonstration of how you want them to learn to behave with others.

Humour

Humour as a de-escalation technique can, if used effectively, work very well. However, sarcasm is not to be used and cannot be used as a humour tool. I have lost count of the number of times I have seen sarcasm used by a teacher, only to then tell off a student for using sarcasm to others in the class or back to the teacher. I have encountered many students who don't understand why it's OK for the teacher to say or do something to a student, but when the student does it back to them it's wrong. Please remember that your students are young people who are experimenting with emotions and how to communicate with each other, and sarcasm always has a victim, as that is the point of it. I have yet to meet a student who hasn't been affected negatively in some way by a sarcastic comment aimed at them. I have had teachers say to me at the start of a lesson observation, *I know you will probably think it's wrong, but I use a lot of sarcasm*. The mere comment shows me that they know that sarcasm can be interpreted by some as unhelpful and hurtful, yet they continue to believe that every student in every class they teach will have the same philosophy as they do, and view sarcasm as a non-emotional tool to make others laugh.

At the end of the lesson, I often have to point out those within the class who didn't say anything again after a comment was aimed at them, and others who didn't venture a comment because of uncertainty about the teacher's response. Yet there were others who loved being part of a group that highlighted the silly things people did or said. Sarcasm has no place within the classroom and should, I believe, be confined to the fantasy world of comedy shows on TV.

Humour can be used to take the seriousness out of a point and disarm comments as it will often cause the person's brain to readjust from the direction they thought the situation was heading. I was watching the Channel 4 documentary *Educating Yorkshire* when one of the girls said that she hated the bloke who invented mathematics. The teacher replied very casually, *'He hates you too'*, which brought a smile and a lightness to a situation that was becoming stressful as they tackled the meaning of algebra.

De-escalation techniques

We all have a natural calm state and there are lots of emotional triggers that will cause us to become annoyed. Understanding what they are and finding techniques to avoid them is a good emotional management tool. Once triggered, some students haven't yet developed ways to de-escalate the situation and get back to their calm state, and that is where you come in with your approach to them within the classroom, or when you perhaps have to have a conversation with them outside the classroom.

CASE STUDY

One student I spoke to about de-escalating the situation put it very well by saying when he gets annoyed it's like he is on an escalator in a shopping centre, and it's taking him to shops that he doesn't want to go to, selling him things like anger, detention, tellings-off from his parents, calls home, and he needs to find ways to avoid that escalator to stay in an area he likes. We came up with an idea that he could have a bookmark simply saying ground floor and second floor and when looking at it, he could visualise the shops on the ground floor selling him things he wants, such as good comments, postcards home to his mum and better grades.

Whatever method you can help the student find, you have to recognise that you can either be the person who helps the student de-escalate or you can be the push in making it worse. You must avoid engaging in power struggles with students – when they make any statement that challenges your authority, let them know that you will continue the conversation at a more appropriate time and you want them to be focusing on the work that needs to be done. For some students, the emotional trigger may have become too embedded and a brief time outside the class, away from the influences of others, may be helpful. Any conversation that you have, even if you are asking a student to leave your class, has to be said in a measured tone so as not to escalate the emotions more.

Critical questions

» What atmosphere do you think you create by being in the room? Do you produce energy, enthusiasm, uncertainty or doubt?

» Do you use humour or have you noticed that sarcasm sometimes creeps in?

» How often do you scan the room to spot those struggling or going off-task?

» Have you considered the impact of your comments on all students within listening distance, not only those you are directly speaking to?

» What form does your detention take? Is it viewed as a time of punishment or a time of reflection and rebuilding?

60-second interview

The three Rs: rewrite the script, rebuild the relationship, refocus the student.

This is a technique I have taught teachers to use when the situation has escalated and they have taken a student out of the classroom to talk to them. It is also very useful in helping the teacher to reflect on their own behaviour and keep calm. Ultimately, you want to build up, maintain and eventually improve the relationship you have with your students and therefore it is important to deal correctly with a situation that is prone to building resentment.

What outcome are you hoping to achieve?

Just think back to your last conversation with a student. Was the conversation driven by your annoyance or by your desire to secure a culture of learning and mutual respect? Whatever the reason, you will already have decided on your choice of approach within the short time-frame between the escalated incident and when both you and the student step outside the door. At exactly the same time as you are deciding which approach to take and what dialogue to use, the student is doing the same.

The 60-second conversation can actually be a very valuable tool in doing all the things mentioned earlier, such as de-escalating the situation, helping engage the thinking brain and calming the emotional brain. First, re-examine the role the student is expecting you to play in this little drama. What script do they think you are bringing to the performance? They will most likely be expecting you to play the 'I know best' role or the 'I am annoyed' role. They will be looking for non-verbal clues; they will focus on your tone of voice as well as your choice of dialogue.

Opening

Rewrite the script: at the opening of your 60-second interview, you therefore have to throw away the script and the role you are desperate to play.

So, for the first few seconds, talk positively about anything you know will interest them and/or be familiar to them. *'How is your sister getting on?', 'How was the weekend?', 'Did your football team win last night?', 'Do you know of a decent fish and chip shop around here?'* Start a casual conversation that is non-threatening and non-confrontational and totally not what they expect. They may try to bring you back to the disruptive behaviour, but you must resist at this point. Use your hand to deflect these comments and ask another question related to your initial enquiry. You are steering the conversation and you are deciding on its composition. In just a few seconds, you will have achieved a calmer and more reasonable dialogue about your chosen subject.

Once they have recognised that you are not going to 'tell them off', you can move into the second part of the interview. Ask them, in a composed and matter-of-fact manner, to describe their learning in this lesson, maybe starting with, *'is there anything you were having difficulty with?'*.

25 seconds

Rebuild the relationship: by now you should be up to about 25 seconds. The student is calmer and you are moving forward in responding to the situation. If they are still very agitated at this stage, then just say, *'I will give you a few moments to think about our conversation so far, as I want to ...'* (whatever you feel you might need to do back in the classroom).

Thank them for the conversation so far. This will do two things. It will give them a chance to reflect upon their behaviour in a more balanced way and it will also give you a chance to get back into the lesson and deal with any fallout.

Dealing with the incident

During the final 35 seconds of the conversation, you need to refer directly to the initial incident in the classroom. At this stage, it wouldn't be uncommon for the student to have already apologised for their behaviour, without any prompting from you. Sometimes, though, there is the need for a gentle enquiry as to why they felt the need to act in that way, when they have proved themselves to be so mature, sensible and understanding in this conversation with you.

It is important now, considering the 60-second window, to secure their future commitment to talking to you about their learning, alongside your assurances to them about making an extra special effort to support them in any way you can.

Back into the classroom

Refocus the student: the final stage is to prepare for the reintegration back into the classroom. Direct them to answer the questions, *What am I going to do when I walk back in? Will I chat to folks?* They will know what you are after and should answer appropriately. Just remember, you are instigating this preparation to ensure the positive atmosphere achieved outside the classroom is not dissolved as soon as they walk back through the classroom door.

As you will appreciate, the 60 seconds is a guide, but it is a good one for keeping you focused and in control of the conversation. Don't cut short the interview if you know you are making progress, but analyse afterwards and see what changes you can make. Eventually the 60-second interview will become a useful tool in helping get students back on track and maintaining or improving the relationship.

Chapter reflections

»   *Your classroom should be a reflection of you and how you want to teach, lead, influence and manage your students. It is an opportunity for you to be a role model of excellence and an influence upon the lives of those who walk to your room for your input throughout the week.*

»   *Your students are expecting things from you and will be receiving not just an academic education but also a social and emotional one – you have to recognise that everything about you will be read by them either subconsciously or consciously.*

»   *View behaviour not as poor or bad, just as inappropriate, and remember that you are the guide, not the disciplinarian to make changes in their choices.*

»   *Develop your techniques to read people and also start to reflect upon yourself, your mannerisms, your tone, as well as other behavioural clues that demonstrate how you are feeling.*

»   *Develop de-escalation techniques to keep students from being triggered and when those triggers have been engaged, look to be the person who finds ways to help your students get back on track.*

»   *As we have recognised, you are working in an emotionally rich environment that can be both rewarding and challenging, and creating an emotionally safe environment goes a long way to helping make your classroom a place worth visiting.*

Taking it further

Cloud, H (2006) *Integrity: The Courage to Meet the Demands of Reality*. New York: Harper Business.

References

Béres, A and Major, T (2011) Does Happiness Help Healing? Immune response of hospitalized children may change during visits of the Smiling Hospital Foundation's Artists. [online] Available at: http://drberesandras-tudomany.blogspot.com (in Hungarian, last accessed 3 July 2017).

Gutman, R (2011) The Untapped Power of Smiling. *Forbes*. [online] Available at: www.forbes.com/sites/ericsavitz/2011/03/22/the-untapped-power-of-smiling (last accessed 20 April 2014).

Helpguide.org (2014) Laughter is the Best Medicine: Health Benefits of Humor and Laughter. [online] Available at: www.helpguide.org/articles/mental-health/laughter-is-the-best-medicine.htm (last accessed 20 June 2018).

Schmidt, K, Levenstein, R and Ambadar, Z (2012) Intensity of Smiling and Attractiveness as Facial Signals of Trustworthiness in Women. *Perceptual and Motor Skills*, 114(3): 964–78.

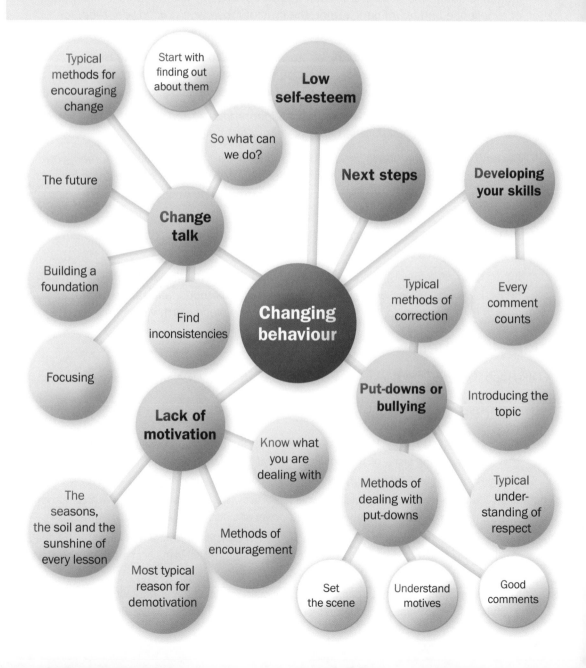

There are no throw-away lines or casual comments when being a teacher, as all will have an impact; that accountability comes with the title 'teacher'.

Author

Introduction

In understanding your students and the variety of emotional and social stimuli continually influencing them, you will inevitably recognise that you need to become knowledgeable about the mind not only as the muscle into which you are inputting academic knowledge but also as the muscle that you are helping train and develop, to enable students to get the best out it for the rest of their lives, and for them to adopt the right mindset for improvement.

By the time we have them in front of us, students' brains will have been influenced by other people, situations, memories and reactions that have become hard-wired to various stimuli. They will inevitably be meeting us with preconceived ideas about how to react and behave to specific things and, more importantly, they will have drawn conclusions about themselves based upon what others have said to them, what they feel and what they have noticed about themselves. This will be a powerful driving force behind how well they are going to achieve.

The conclusions they reach may be positive and uplifting just as they may be debilitating and disabling; either way, it is what we will have to work with, so no matter what mindset they have, we need to nurture it to be one of hope, belief in themselves and forward thinking. Only when those things are in place will we be able to get them to fully engage in achieving the best they possibly can.

I am going to deal with some of the issues that you will inevitably come across within your class as these have a very negative impact and are unfortunately very common. These topics are 'put-downs' or bullying, lack of motivation and low self-esteem. Unfortunately, these three issues are on the increase. But, like all problems, they are just waiting for a solution – we need to be a part of that solution. So before we look at each of these issues, I want first to talk about developing your skills more generally.

Developing your skills

As a teacher, we are also in an enviable position of being a learner; I love the statement 'every day is a school day', as we need to look at what the world and those within it are teaching us.

There are lots of negative situations out there, but often the jewels of insight and understanding are hidden within them. As teachers we will inevitably come across those jewels of knowledge or insights from our students that help us understand better, empathise better and therefore teach better.

So the things that I am outlining here are for you to try out, hone and develop with your students, listening to what they say in response to your questions and getting feedback from them, so that you can create that positive emotional environment within your classroom which helps strengthen the mental well-being of all, enabling them to achieve a more positive outlook on themselves and others.

Every comment counts

I want first for us all to recognise the importance of everything we say to our students, every interaction that we have with them, as well as the importance of how we act when we are not with students.

You have to get used to the idea that you will be watched, observed and assessed, from the moment you arrive at school, when you teach, when you walk in the corridor, when you are on duty, when you are often not aware of it. The students are going to be interested in you, and you are worth taking notice of as a teacher.

You are therefore on duty all the time and you can undo the good that you are aiming to achieve inside the classroom by an unguarded moment and a casual statement that gets interpreted the wrong way outside of the classroom.

You are teaching more than academic subjects to those you come into contact with. Leadership skills, social skills and how to act as an adult are all there for others to learn from you. It is more real than reality TV will ever be, as during your career you will have an audience of tens of thousands, and you will be making an impression on all those you seek to influence.

CASE STUDY

A while ago, I travelled with a group of students with their support workers in a minibus. As we drove to the park where we were taking them for the day to work on their social skills, when asked to turn up the radio because the students in the back wanted to listen to it, one of the support workers decided that they would turn the radio up and then down for the next 30 seconds 'as a joke'.

The students were there because they had to be taken out of normal lessons due to their poor ability to control their interaction with each other. They were being given advice in small-group settings about how to treat each other with empathy and respect, but instead they had a valuable lesson from the support worker about how to annoy others. The students then aimed a range of comments at the support workers – unfortunately none of the kind I was hoping to encourage.

When I spoke with the support worker about it I was told to 'relax' and 'chill' and take time off as it was a day trip. It is often the interpretation that worthwhile learning is confined to a structured lesson within the classroom, and the rest of the time can be less focused. But learning is not confined to a room or a timetable, and we have not only to get used to being at work within a lesson but also to be aware of the implications of what we do and say at other times, especially for those who are more emotionally vulnerable and who may have even fewer skills in interpreting our comments and actions.

Critical questions

» *Does your behaviour vary depending on where you are around school?*

» *Have you reflected upon the impact of your statements?*

» *Are you aware of using comments and statements outside the classroom to reinforce your expected behaviour within?*

Put-downs or bullying

I often get asked by teachers, *'how do you stop the students saying such nasty things about each other?'.* Bullying can be a very destructive process and usually isn't confined to one comment, as the initial comment leads to retaliation, which, in turn, will encourage others to take sides and add their own comment. Before you know it, a single sentence has divided the class and can have repercussions that spill out of your lesson, and is very hard to address it just by telling students to stop.

Typical methods of correction

Punishment isn't a good tool to employ when trying to teach empathy. It also sometimes gives the person who is being punished a feeling of pride in what they have done. Appealing to them to take into account the feelings of others also tends to fall on deaf ears as they are not that interested in the feelings of others during the period of their lives when brain activity is encouraging them to become independent. A recent study tracked the 'cognitive empathy' of teens over time. During the teenage years, the capacity for empathy that has developed from a very early age tends to take a nose dive, as the brain seeks to establish its own place in the world, to take control of situations and to be more selfish in its outlook (Van der Graaff et al, 2014).

The negativity that these comments create and the frequency with which they occur often means that you cannot deal with them in just a few moments. You are dealing with a variety of reasons for the behaviour and expecting those involved to consciously choose to behave in an alternative manner to what comes naturally by impulse. Not surprisingly, therefore, it has to be dealt with at a time when people are calm and the issues can be discussed rationally.

How many times have you had to 'bite your tongue'? That is a good study to show the amount of control one needs not to say something. So to expect a young emotionally immature student to possess such maturity without coaching and guidance is unrealistic.

Introducing the topic

It is always good if you can start by stating at the outset of your time with the students that within your class there is going to be an expectation from everyone to treat each other with respect. Please be aware that just saying this without understanding what they mean by 'respect' is a waste of your time, as your understanding and theirs can be vastly different.

Typical understanding of respect

CASE STUDY

I met with a group of boys in school who had started to form a gang, and after a few weeks, I asked them what they thought about the word respect. The standard answer was that they 'respect those who respect them'.

I asked them if they respected me and they said yes. I then asked them why, when we first met together, they went into my box of initiative games and, on finding some sweets there, had a few from the bag without asking me or telling me they had done so? The response was that they were only sweets and weren't worth much; they wouldn't have taken anything expensive. To which I said, 'So your respect has a monetary value then?'

I then asked about their respect for the building and the cleaning staff who clean up after them as they leave litter and mess, and they said 'They get paid for doing that so it's their job'. *So I said, 'You don't necessarily need to respect the state of a building as someone will clean it up, as that's their job and they get money, so you don't have to take into consideration the impact on others.'*

I then asked, 'What about if someone volunteered to clean things, would you then have respect for the building and the person who has to tidy up after you?' They said, 'If they're doing the job for nothing then it proves that they are idiots and we don't respect stupid people.'

I asked them about their respect for each other and they said that they respected each other and always looked out for each other if it came to a fight. I asked, 'What about when not in a fight situation, what about the respect for when someone tries to do something and gets it wrong, when do you encourage and show respect for each other?' They said that they just had a laugh and a joke and they didn't need to show respect as it was always there in the background.

I then said, 'Let me just check I have got your understanding of respect correct. You respect those who respect you, a philosophy you live by, but there are exceptions, such as anyone's small monetary possession – even though you respect them, you can take without asking or mentioning. You don't need to respect rooms and places you visit as people will clean up after you for money, or if they are volunteers then they don't get respect as they are idiots and you don't respect idiots. As for friends, you respect them even though most of the time you are saying negative things to each other, but that is OK, because when you ever find yourselves in a fight you will look after each other. Is that what you mean by the word respect?'

After that conversation we spent time talking about the true meaning of respect and looking at changing the way they talked to each other. We looked at times when they could show respect to each other, and encourage one another, and we practised saying nice things about each other. They found this both strange and uncomfortable, which emphasised the point that, to them, it was easier to make others look bad, as this was a way to make themselves feel good.

Methods of dealing with put-downs

Set the scene

As the teacher, you have to lead by example in being the one who shows empathy and respect. If you engage in any process that involves the development of emotional intelligence without first being a person who demonstrates it, you are unlikely to be successful.

Understand motives

We must always understand the motives of the person making the comment. This in itself could have a variety of reasons, and your first task is to find out that motivating reason for the people involved. With the group of boys I dealt with, their motives were that it was a source of amusement for them and a time for them to feel good about themselves at the expense of one of their own. It had become a socially acceptable part of the group to sometimes be the victim and other times the instigator of the derogatory comments. Yet they admitted that they would prefer not to do it, and this was what formed the basis of the change in attitude to each other.

So you can start the discussion with the group or class by asking them to think about the times when they have said something about another person and to think about the possible motives behind it. List the reasons on the board as they will form the basis of the examination within the group. Ask them to think about the most hurtful thing that someone has said to them and to describe how it felt physically. Sometimes it can be useful to ask them to walk across the room demonstrating the body language associated with that feeling, so that you can see that it affects the body as well as the mind.

Ask them to think about the worst things that they have said to others and lead the conversation towards the fact that the aim is often to make others feel bad and that this in some way makes us feel good.

Good comments

Ask them now to think of a good comment that they have either given or received. Get them to share that in groups or in the whole class. Ask them to describe how it made them feel. This also can be acted out.

Ask them to think how much time is spent saying bad things about others as opposed to saying good things. What are the thoughts that prevent them from saying good things about each other?

The aim is to have a good open discussion and to highlight that we have all, at some point in our lives, had unkind things said about us or to us, and, even though we have felt the pain and even remember the feeling long after the event, we have also at times been the author of such comments to others.

Yet we also have the capacity within us to bring encouragement and kindness that will remain with us and those with whom we share it long after the words have been said. (While I was writing this, the postman delivered a letter from a person I worked with over two years ago.

She had written to the school to which she was going at the time requesting they pass the letter on to me. In it she wrote: *'Thank you so much for believing in me when my world was filled with fear and doubt.'*)

Within the lesson, you can then ask the students to act out different scenarios, such as someone getting the wrong answer to a question that others might find easy, or someone not liking the same programme or group as others. The point here is to make it as realistic as you can, and you can act out some that you may have seen within other classes that you have taught.

These scenarios will help students to recognise that the words they use in these situations are an attempt to make them feel good about themselves or show off at the expense of others.

Then you can ask them to explore how they can feel good about themselves at the same time as making the other person feel good. Remember that saying something nice about others will not come easily to some, and the thought of doing so, as we have already seen, carries with it assumptions that prevent this from happening. Yet it is these assumptions that you are challenging, as well as the impact of the negativity.

The more honest the students are about the negative effects of bad comments at the beginning, the more the reality of the situation is brought home and change is encouraged. Those feelings of hurt and frustration that negativity causes can be a powerful tool in helping you create a negative-free zone, first of all within your classroom, and then by encouraging students to aim to make their lives a negative-free zone as well.

Critical questions

» *Have you asked the people involved to comment upon reasons for their actions?*

» *What types of things do you say and what has been the effect?*

» *Have you spent time encouraging good behaviour and comments?*

Whenever you get rid of a bad habit it needs to be replaced with something else, so this is a good time to introduce the 'Noticed Board'. Suggest to students the idea that you would like to include the Noticed Board, and that at certain points during your lesson you will quickly ask them to name someone who has made a good impression on them, contributed well to the lesson, helped them, shared, encouraged, supported. Write the headings up at the start and ask them to be looking out for this throughout the time together. If they want to, they can include things that happened outside of the lesson.

You can develop the idea as you wish as you get to know your students, but it will help toward contributing to a positive, more inclusive atmosphere and also to highlighting more effectively whenever anyone makes a negative comment, as this becomes increasingly out of place.

Highlighting the topic and dealing with it in such a full-on way is by far the best way to encourage change, as the discussion is led and directed by the students talking about their feelings, their reactions and the effects upon them, yet you are being the guide and encourager to enable them to approach things with a different mindset.

The environment you are seeking to create has to become one where people feel capable of making mistakes without the fear of negativity, as well as one where those who want to succeed can flourish without being thought of as different from the others.

Lack of motivation

The lack of motivation to even try from some students can be very draining, but it is important to recognise the methods we use to encourage them to try as well as to look at the contributing factors.

The seasons, the soil and the sunshine of every lesson

We talked in Chapter 4 about the need for the 3 Ms: Model, Manageable and Meaningful. All lessons need those three main ingredients for success. A simple way to remember them is to think of them as the seasons, the soil and the sunshine within your classroom that enable your students to grow and succeed, just as they enable plants to grow.

Getting these things right helps build confidence and therefore engagement.

*   **Seasons.** For things to happen in an orderly, expected way, just like the season, the students need to know what is going to happen within your lessons. Are you familiar and consistent with them so there are no surprises or contradictions? Just like plant life suffers when seasons are out of kilter, your students will suffer if you are not consistent.

*   **Soil.** Do your students feel they can manage what is being asked of them, or at least that you are able to help them appropriately? Do they feel that they are in the right environment to grow and flourish, just as it is important for a plant to have the right soil to feed it?

*   **Sunshine.** Finally, are the lessons bringing purpose and meaning which encourages students to stretch and grow just like plants in the sunshine?

Without these three things, students suffer and become demotivated. Just like a plant, if any one of these is missing then you will notice the plant withering; sometimes the students you are teaching are slumped on the desk and no encouragement from you seems to rouse them.

Most typical reason for demotivation

The most typical reason I have come across for demotivation is the third one of the three (sunshine) being absent from the classroom. Quite often, students are unable to see the point of the lesson and, as discussed earlier, it's important that you explore their own motivation to see how you can make the lesson relevant to them.

Methods of encouragement

Your encouragement and enthusiasm will be important to the atmosphere within the class; just as you are influenced by others, so you can have an influence. At times when motivation and enthusiasm are low, you have to provide it. The influence of smiles and tone of voice will go some way to helping those who have embedded themselves into negativity.

Know what you are dealing with

What is the person's diet like? What are their sleep patterns like? No matter how enthusiastic you are, if someone has had only a few hours' sleep and no food, you are going to struggle. As in all situations, finding out as much information as you can about what the person is thinking and doing outside of school will give you some idea as to why they are behaving the way they do within school.

It is increasingly becoming a problem that students are staying awake until the early hours playing games or chatting on their phones. Check to see what are the sleeping patterns for those who are finding it hard to stay on task. It is also fairly common for students not to have breakfast and this can be a problem for some who perhaps have had to stay behind in the lesson during first break, making it impossible for them to get anything to eat. If this happens it could mean that they have gone without food for 18 hours by the time lunchtime comes. The young brain especially will find it harder to cope emotionally and academically if this is happening.

The other factor to consider is the onset of adolescence and the way this also affects the behaviour of young people and students. In his book *Surviving Your Child's Adolescence*, Carl Pickhardt (2013) speaks about the five realities that young people go through that affect them emotionally and socially through adolescence. This includes a negative mindset and this can also be linked to drop in academic achievement as a young person searches for meaning and things that truly interest them rather than what adults have been directing them towards.

Critical questions

» *How often do you monitor the seasons, the soil and the sunshine throughout your lessons?*

» *Do you ask the students what they think about the order, manageability and purpose of the lesson?*

» *Notice the next time you get bored while doing something and see which of the three you have found wanting.*

» *Have you asked them about their sleep and eating pattern?*

» *Have you noticed a shift in their overall work and commitment towards school as they potentially seek new direction?*

Low self-esteem

Self-esteem is based on confidence in one's own worth or ability. Therefore low self-esteem can have tremendously debilitating effects on an adolescent's self-perception. It is also widely believed to have a negative impact on health, behaviour and prospects in later adult life. As a teacher, you will constantly hear comments like *'I can't do that'* or *'I'm no good at that'* from students. Their failure to attempt tasks, sometimes appearing as a lack of motivation, may in fact be part of confirming their own negative feelings about themselves: *I am not very good at things and therefore it's not even worth trying, as all it will do is prove the point that I am going to fail.*

These views about themselves are formed at an early age when they are ill-equipped to look at comments objectively and are strongly influenced by those around them, often people they look up to or have a close relationship with. Anything that continually reinforces their negativity about themselves may form the foundation on which they view everything in the future. These early experiences could include failure to meet parents' expectations and standards, punishment, neglect or abuse, an absence of praise, warmth or affection, or belittling comments or unfair comparison to other family members or friends. The origins of these negative beliefs are not just confined to the formative years but they may also be caused by experiences later in life through poor relationships or even workplace bullying.

What it comes down to is that a person suffering from this negative view of themselves is viewing life from the wrong viewpoint. No matter how often you tell them otherwise, this is the view they have.

The starting point for any of the change that needs to occur is for you to help the person focus on their strengths and what they are good at. You must also keep demonstrating that sense of belief and confidence in them and not waver. When you are talking with them, remember that your tone of voice as well as what you say will have a part to play. You should try to be calm, matter of fact and logical in what you are saying, as emotion and encouragement is often seen as you 'being nice'. I remember one child saying that she never believed what a teacher said in praise, as they were meant to say such things as part of their job.

Low self-esteem can also be linked to the changes a young person goes through during their adolescence. They don't like how they look, and they are becoming more self-conscious during stages of puberty. It is important to keep an eye on someone who has a negative mindset who might also be on the receiving end of teasing and bullying, as a negativity towards the self combined with negativity from others can have lasting effects at this vulnerable age. Self-rejection and social rejection can be very hard to bear.

CASE STUDY

I was once talking to a student about a piece of artwork and asked if they were pleased with it. When they said, 'No, it's crap', I said, 'Fair enough. On your scale of crap is it the best crap you have done or have you done worse?' And when they said they had done worse I asked them what made this piece better than the other piece. We then had a chat about how they viewed things.

It is important to remember that you need to start from where they are and, if possible, get them to realign their perspective on things. This will then open up the conversation to how they view themselves.

The more you can encourage them to say good things about themselves the better. You may be just a small part in helping them change their view, but it might just be the start they need. Do the opposite of what they have experienced and make your praise and compliments relative to the amount of effort and quality they have achieved. When I hear teachers using the words *amazing* or *brilliant* for mediocre work or little effort, I often ask what they would say when the student actually does something amazing and brilliant.

I have also had to talk with another teacher who never gave high marks to a specific student as he felt that it might make him stop trying. When I asked the student how he felt about his marks, he told me that no matter how hard he tried, it was never good enough for the teacher, so he had now given up trying. Make your methods meet the needs of the individual.

Critical questions

»   *What methods of praise do you use to encourage students?*

»   *Are you sometimes overly critical to encourage a student to do better without taking into account their needs?*

»   *Do you find yourself arguing the opposite rather than starting from where the students see themselves?*

»   *Do you praise the person or just the work?*

»   *Do you gloss over the good work to push towards improvements rather than celebrating the success?*

»   *When talking with a student, do you see them as they are or as what they can become?*

»   *When dealing with a student with low self-esteem, do you check on their friendship network as well?*

Change talk

Your conversations are aiming to help students examine their approach to their lives as well as the lessons, and, where appropriate, can help guide them to alternative approaches.

The technique I use has grown out of motivational interview techniques developed by William R Miller and Stephen Rollnick (2002) that involve a collaborative, goal-orientated style of communication with particular attention paid to the language of change. They are used to strengthen a person's motivation for commitment to a specific goal by exploring that person's own reason for change. The aim is to do this in a non-judgemental and accepting environment. The concept of motivational interviewing evolved from experience in the treatment of problem drinkers was first described by Miller (1983) in an article published in *Behavioural Psychotherapy*, and has since developed into a recognised form of counselling.

I have adapted it to work within the coaching arena within schools as a method of exploring ambivalence and challenging students to examine their approach to issues and problems, taking into account the age and development of the brain.

Put simply, the concept as taught by Miller and Rollnick is that people themselves are the main instigators of change and it is their own ideas and thoughts that prevent them from actually changing.

Find inconsistencies

When talking to anyone behaving in a way that is unhelpful to themselves your aim is to find out the reasons why, and look to see if there are areas within what they are saying that are in fact inconsistent with what they want.

As I outlined earlier with the students who thought they understood respect and knew how to demonstrate it, asking them questions highlighted to them that in fact they were doing the opposite of respecting themselves and others, especially their friends. Once they had reached that realisation, it was the time to introduce to them the idea of changing their approach to things.

Typical methods for encouraging change

In their book *Motivational Interviewing*, Miller and Rollnick outline the typical methods that people use to try to elicit change, and they include the most common that I hear when in school. These can be categorised into arguing for change, using punishment or threats of bad things happening if they don't change, or giving rewards if they do.

All of these methods are often met with little or no positive effect. Any effect that is elicited is often only temporary while the motivating factor is present. That is why punishment, or the threat of punishment, is so often revisited, or rewards have to keep being given as an incentive, and when they don't work, then arguments about what will happen to them and the negative response from the students tend to follow.

So what can we do?

Be realistic in what you are able to achieve to start with, but make sure that you are consistent in your approach with the student as you help them explore how and why they are so demotivated. The conversations that you have are aimed at students discovering for themselves the positive reason for change and examining what they are doing at the moment that in fact is the opposite, or at least inconsistent with, what they want or hope for.

Put aside your comments about what they should do, or how they should behave, what they should be thinking, and also any comments about how you used to be at their age, especially the ones that start with *'I was just like you'*. You may well have been, but if you remember back then, you will also remember that adults telling you what to do and giving you advice about how to behave and think was very annoying.

Start with finding out about them

CASE STUDY

I once asked a student who was having problems with his behaviour within school what he hoped to do. Now I know that this question is tricky for a lot of teenagers; either they don't know or have a unrealistic expectation of what they want. I ask it as the answer will give me a good indication of how they see their future.

The answer on this occasion was, 'I am going to end up in prison.'

I needed to relate to what he was saying and thinking, so I told him that that was an option and ask how long he was planning on going for. A short few weeks, months, or was he looking for years? What kind of crime had he looked in to? I said I could understand it was an option as he would get to meet like-minded people there, receive regular meals and health checks, and possibly might even be able to pick up on some education. I said it was an interesting career option. I also said I would prefer it if he went to college but it was his choice.

I then asked him why he thought it was better than college. Had people said he would end up in prison? It turned out that that was where the thoughts originated – someone had tried to encourage him to change by scaring him with the possibility that if he stayed the same he would end up in prison. They had not been able to provide him with any help as to how to change, so he was left with the inevitable conclusion that prison was where he was heading.

We then had a discussion about what alternatives he had looked at, and what he had tried to do in the past. What had been the stumbling blocks? What things beyond his control did he need help with and what things could he try to change himself with support?

Slowly we worked at a strategy that he could believe in, that he owned and took responsibility for, that, with the staff's help (no longer telling him what to do but offering support), he could achieve.

After we had put this strategy together and he could start to see the light at the end of the tunnel, I asked him what I had done to help him. He thought for a moment and then said 'nothing'. He realised that he had done it all and I had just provided the conversation for him to get started and helping him believe he could do things.

The process you are following, then, is first to get to know the student and the issue that they are facing. You can then learn what concerns them about themselves and their future, if they have any hopes and dreams. All the time you are asking these questions, you are interested in their answers and not adding your comments and thoughts or interpretations on what they are saying. Let them tell you, let them have the freedom to explore what they actually do think about the answers.

For some very negative students the process can be very slow and the answers may be very short. But remember this is no reason to give up – it is all the more reason to be positive and encouraging about how you ask the questions, knowing that your tone will be having a positive effect upon their brain.

Focusing

What you are trying to do is to look for the point where they highlight things that they would like to change. I haven't yet met a teenager who doesn't want to improve his or her lot within school; it is just that some are ill-equipped to do so.

Sometimes the simple question, *what one thing would you like to be different?* is enough for them to focus on the possibilities that things could be better. The lack of motivation and ability to change often stems from the thought that they have so much that they have to change and get right. Yet with all things, if it's worth doing it's worth starting and it's worth the journey. I remind students that the brain is used to trying and succeeding when things are difficult, but over time those difficult things become normal. Learning to walk is full of falls and difficulties but can be learnt with determination and help from others.

Ask your students to think of how they would feel if they could do something. Who would they tell if they had a good a lesson? What would they say?

You are aiming to get them to start mentally considering that change is possible and the results of those changes will be beneficial for them and also will have a good effect upon those for whom they care.

I was once asked to work with a student who refused to do any work within mathematics and hadn't done any for weeks. I spent an hour with him, and over that hour we talked and he drew one triangle. For the teacher this was nothing, and on the scale of things, it was very poor. Yet to him, he *had* achieved something in that hour, and I made a big thing of it in a joking way, but in a way that meant he was smiling and ended the lesson being con-gratulated rather than feeling bad about himself. It was the start, and for some who start so far back, any movement forward is better than the direction in which they have been travelling.

These conversations take time and may have to be done outside of the lesson-appointed time, but the method will still be the same: get to know them and then look for anything in what they have said that you can focus upon as they aim for improvement.

Once that has been established and they can focus upon something they are going to change, then see what support they will need to help them and ask them what things they can see might be stumbling blocks. Enlisting their friends at this point is a good move to help keep up the enthusiasm and encouragement.

Building a foundation

Keep asking students what they are thinking and get them to say as many encouraging things about the process as you can. Get their friends to also speak words of encouragement and mention the importance of a good support structure and friends that look out for them. Letters home highlighting any improvements will hopefully mean that positive comments can be added there as well.

The foundation will be tried and there will often be relapses into lethargy or poor behaviour, but this is not to be focused upon; the emphasis on what has been achieved is always the important point. Just as a child walking their first few steps may get the biggest round of applause, it does not mean that the child has perfected it. There will be many a fall and scraped knee, but a dutiful parent or guardian is there to pick them up and help them start again.

The analogy is just as appropriate for the teenager trying to change a negative attitude. You will need to look out for and help them avoid the things that will cause them to stumble and regress, but always be vigilant to provide encouragement and praise. Those small steps of improvements will soon be turning into a longer journey. The hope is that they can do so within your oversight so they can progress with their education and life.

The future

Once the change has become a little more established, then practical and achievable goals can be set. These may have to involve their lifestyle as well as their academic lives.

I am working with a group of Year 11 students and trying to encourage them to engage their thinking brain as they enter the classroom in which they have been disruptive for the last two years. I often have to point out to them that drinking a can of energy drink as well as eating a bar of chocolate will hinder what they are telling me they want to achieve.

I explain to them it's like entering a race fully prepared and, just before you set off, you tie your laces together. No matter what the crowd does in cheering for you, or the coach does in preparing you, you are going to trip up. But I also add that it is their choice, and if they want my help they can always have it, but tripping themselves up will just make things a bit harder and a bit trickier and longer.

I then ask them what they are thinking. The usual answer is that they have always done it that way. That is the rut that a lot of people have got themselves into and they need help, support and encouragement to get out of it. And sometimes those attitudes are in short supply because their very actions have over time led people to believe that what is left for them is punishment and a hope that in some way they will change their behaviour.

Poor motivation or apathy towards change can have many reasons behind it, but the important thing is for you to have the belief in your students and provide them with the motivation to get things moving first of all. Remember, you are the leader, the visionary and the enabler on so many different issues, and the students, just like that plant, might need some good soil, water and sunshine to start to revive again.

Critical questions

» *What methods have been used upon you to encourage you to change your behaviour?*

» *Did they work or were they a tool to enable self-reflection?*

» *What methods do you use to encourage change?*

»   *Have you ever advised rather than listened?*

»   *Can you think of students whom you can encourage to talk about what they want to try rather than advising them what to do?*

Chapter reflections

»   *What you say and do outside of the lesson can have an impact upon what goes on within a lesson. You are at work all the time and the environment that you create within the classroom has a lot to do with how you are outside of it.*

»   *To enable the students to grow into emotionally competent, socially responsible adults within your classroom, as well as outside, you might have to spend some of your time dealing with those issues that cause discord and stunt both learning and growth. Let the students be the instruments for their own change and be the leaders in how they should approach things.*

»   *Highlight what you are looking for and the reasons you are looking for it. Remember to create an environment that contains encouragement of each other. Get them to notice good things and join you in commenting upon them. This will go some way to dealing with poor motivation within your classroom.*

»   *All this will, like most things, take time, but be consistent with your approach. Build a relationship with those who have low motivation and lots of apathy, focus on what is possible, lay a foundation of improvement and work towards a future that is good for them.*

»   *All of the above are part of the working year and can be dealt with either before things arise or once you have noticed them occurring. Dealing with issues about bullying and negative comments is best tackled early, before resentment or poor behaviour has become embedded. Develop your technique and over time it will become the norm and the expectation of you as a teacher.*

»   *Food and drink, as well as lack of sleep, will impact upon the students at this age and there are lots of things that are taking their attention at night with the ability to contact others through social network sites.*

»   *Trying to take away things they enjoy doing or are part of their culture will only work if they are replaced by things they can equally enjoy, feel good about or see the benefit in doing. This will always come down to how well you know your students, so keep building relationships over the time with them.*

Next steps

For some within the class, the pressures of the world and the difficulties that it brings are compounded because of the special needs with which they are also having to deal. We will look at some of the things that you can do to help you manage them within your classroom in the next chapter.

References

Miller, W R (1983) Motivational Interviewing with Problem Drinkers. *Behavioural Psychotherapy*, 11: 147–72.

Miller, W R and Rollnick, S (2002) *Motivational Interviewing: Preparing people for change*. New York: Guilford Publications.

Pickhardt, C E (2013) *Surviving Your Child's Adolescence: How to Understand, and Even Enjoy, the Rocky Road to Independence*. San Francisco, CA: Jossey-Bass.

Van der Graaff, J et al (2014) Perspective Taking and Empathic Concern in Adolescence: Gender Differences in Developmental Changes. *Developmental Psychology*, 50(3): 881–8.

8 Support staff and special educational needs

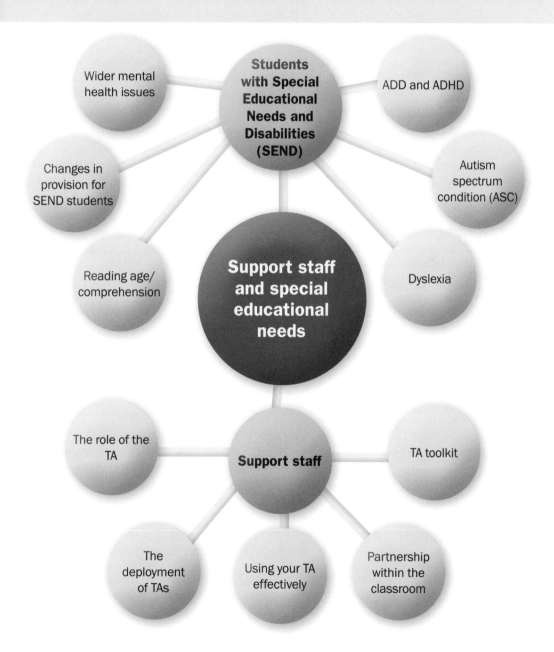

Introduction

The last few chapters have looked at some typical emotional issues that students within your lessons may face, and the need for you to take into account the influence you can have in helping them grow as emotionally intelligent adults with the skills needed to learn and contribute effectively to society.

Yet you will undoubtedly come across other students within your teaching career who have special educational needs and disabilities (SEND) and therefore need to be treated differently. Developing your knowledge and skills in these areas will go a long way in also developing your skills with the other students, as they will require you to think more intently about your input, teaching methods and measuring outcomes.

You may have support in the classroom from teaching assistants (TAs) and additional support from the school SEN department, including the Special Educational Needs Co-ordinator (SENCo) and Inclusion Manager (IM), whose role is to line manage the TAs, prepare and monitor their timetables and support the day-to-day running of the SEN department. The time of a SENCo is often spread over the important aspects of writing reports for students with Educational Health Care Plans (EHCPs) and liaising with the Educational Psychologists, as well as often having a teaching load as well. So it is important to develop your own skills and find information about working with students with special needs and disabilities from any quarter you can.

Critical questions

»   *What SEN information do you know about students within your class?*

»   *How are the TAs allocated around the school?*

»   *What specialist knowledge does your TA have about the students within your class?*

Students with Special Educational Needs and Disabilities (SEND)

ADD and ADHD

The various categories that will need to be considered are attention deficit disorder (ADD) and attention deficit hyperactivity disorder (ADHD). There has been a definite rise in the diagnosis of this disorder: *'Prescriptions for the drug methylphenidate (Ritalin) used in the management of childhood and adult ADHD (attention deficit hyperactivity disorder) have grown by 56 per cent over the six-year period since 2007'* (Broyd, 2013).

Even if the student is on medication, they will still need your understanding of how they learn best and the processes you need to go through to get the best out of them.

Students with ADHD find it difficult to be calm and still. To help with this, your SENCo may have issued them with some kind of twiddler or squeezy toy. These are small stress relievers that can be twiddled with unobtrusively to keep the student focused and their hands off others' possessions! Other students (including those with ADD) find a 'doodle' book helps, rather than defacing their schoolbooks and getting into trouble.

If you notice problems with an ADD student who has previously been settled, check with your IM whether there are issues at home. It may be (especially during Year 9) that their hormones have kicked in or they have had a growth spurt and so may need their medication reassessed. Remember, too, that these students' brains may be developing at different levels. They will most likely be socialising with younger students, so you will need to account for this immaturity when putting them into groups to work in your class.

Keep your instructions succinct, break up their work into smaller chunks and give them time-related objectives. Where possible, use a little timer on their desk or an online countdown timer for the whole class. Another idea is to have small starter tasks (related to your subject) to allow them a five-minute 'break' with something fun related; an hour of one lesson is a lot for sufferers of ADD. They can then return to their original set work with renewed focus.

Autism spectrum condition (ASC)

Autism and Asperger syndrome are both part of a range of related developmental disorders known as autism spectrum condition (ASC) (NHS, 2013). The reason for the word 'spectrum' is there are varying levels of severity of autism and Asperger syndrome. Students with these disorders suffer from a triad of impairments: social communication, social interaction and social imagination (National Autistic Society, 2014a). You can probably assume that if the student is in your mainstream school then their condition is manageable. However, they will still struggle with communication and interacting with others, which can lead to anxiety and confusion. Again, you should check with your IM whether the student is on medication and has set strategies to use, as each individual will have different ways of responding and dealing with their days in school. Building a relationship with these students is very important for you to understand how to manage their learning and behaviour with as few problems as possible.

Most students with these disorders will respond positively to clear, unambiguous instructions. However, it is crucial that if you say you are going to do something a certain way that you do it that way, as they do not like or understand change. If something is to be changed, let them know as much in advance as possible and explain why it has been changed.

One of the main issues of those with ASC is their apparent lack of empathy with others and their lack of social understanding of situations (National Autistic Society, 2014a). This can lead to problems with their peers, so you need to be aware of this when placing groups together.

Students with Asperger syndrome are usually higher-level achievers of above average intelligence, and do not usually have the learning disabilities connected to autism (National Autistic Society, 2014b). They still struggle with social relationships and lack of empathy, but they can generally handle their issues more easily, with support and guidance from trained adults, and lead full and independent lives.

Dyslexia

Students in your lessons who have difficulty learning to read fluently and with accurate comprehension may need to be tested by your IM. Do not assume that all who have this difficulty are dyslexic, as often there are other phonological and processing difficulties. However, if they do have a diagnosis they should be having regular support from your SEND team. Within your lessons you can:

- print work on buff or pastel paper (this reduces glare and helps to 'fix' the words on the page);

- use coloured overlays and/or reading rulers which allow the student to see just a sentence or small paragraph at a time;

- ensure your student can read black on white from your whiteboard; often blue is better;

- some fonts are easier to read than others; check with the student or your IM which are best for your student.

Your relationship is again key to knowing what your student is comfortable with within the class. Removing stress and anxiety simply by understanding that, for example, they dread being asked to read aloud, will change their whole attitude to you and attending your lesson.

Changes in provision for SEND students

The different categories associated with SEND and what the terms refer to will, to begin with, seem daunting, and the list of acronyms that you will have to get used to within the educational sector is immense. (Legislation is in the process of changing the named categories. However, whatever the name they choose to give it, the students will fall basically within the same categories and your SENCo will be able to give you information about the changes that have taken place since 2014.)

Critical questions

» *Do you know who to go to find information relating to your SEND students?*

» *Can you access relevant information relating to individual students within your school and how easy is it?*

» *What noticeable differences would you expect to see within your class between autism and Asperger syndrome?*

» *Have you changed the print paper colour to take into account the needs of your students?*

» *What guidelines would you think are appropriate when placing someone with ASD in a group?*

Reading age/comprehension

Some students within the class may have a reading age well below the national average and therefore may be unable to understand written material contained within textbooks or even written examples that you provide to explain what needs to be done.

Equally, some may read well but have little comprehension of the story being told or information being provided within the text. Ensure comprehension by frequently asking the young person or student to explain what has been read.

At the start of your time with any new class or new students, it is vital that you familiarise yourself with their reading age and match the written material accordingly for them. PowerPoint slides for the whole class may be effective, but it is important to consider the student with SEND when creating them. It might be advisable to print off a copy of the slides personally for the TA so they can refer to them as you move through the presentation for the class. The lower reading age, the more graphics students like to see and this is also important when it comes to things like handouts.

A quick and easy way to familiarise yourself with the ability of specific reading ages is to look at books within the library at the relevant ages and see the sentence structure and words used. You will see how quickly accessing the learning can become a problem for those who are of low reading ability. It is vital to meet the needs of these students, otherwise the only recourse left for some students is to misbehave, as this is a great way of avoiding the embarrassment of the fact that they can't read very well.

The techniques and methods that have already been mentioned in the earlier chapters will go a long way in helping to meet these needs, and the TA and the SENCo will be able to offer advice regarding differentiation.

Basic strategies to consider include:

* making sure the text is relevant to their reading age;
* pairing with a more able student if you have to read or explain something to the whole class;
* developing a peer role-model system;
* clearly differentiating work set when working together;
* making sure the pace of lesson is appropriate for all;
* using a variety of media;
* providing pre-defined pictures that help explain things;
* setting realistic, achievable homework and supporting students who find the task of working without support extremely difficult.

Wider mental health issues

ADD, ADHD, ASD and dyslexia actually only form a small proportion of the issues associated with mental health that you may come across. Here are some facts about the wider mental health issues affecting young people.

- *1 in 10 children and young people aged 5–16 suffer from a diagnosable mental health disorder – that is around three children in every class. (Nuffield Foundation, 2013)*

- *Between 1 in 12 and 1 in 15 children and young people deliberately self-harm. (Mental Health Foundation, 2006)*

- *There has been a big increase in the number of young people being admitted to hospital because of self-harm. Over the last ten years this figure has increased by 68 per cent. (YoungMinds, 2011)*

- *More than half of all adults with mental health problems were diagnosed in childhood. Less than half were treated appropriately at the time. (Kim-Cohen et al, 2003)*

- *Nearly 80,000 children and young people suffer from severe depression. (Green et al, 2005)*

- *Over 8,000 children under 10 years old suffer from severe depression. (Green et al, 2005)*

- *72 per cent of children in care (looked after children – LAC) have behavioural or emotional problems – these are some of the most vulnerable people in our society. (Sempik et al, 2008)*

- *95 per cent of imprisoned young offenders have a mental health disorder. Many of them are struggling with more than one disorder. (Office for National Statistics, 1997)*

- *The number of young people aged 15–16 with depression nearly doubled between the 1980s and the 2000s. (Collishaw et al, 2004)*

- *The proportion of young people aged 15–16 with a conduct disorder more than doubled between 1974 and 1999. (Collishaw et al, 2004)*

(YoungMinds, 2014)

Whatever the estimate is for mental health disorders, the likelihood of it manifesting itself within your class needs to be taken into account when you are planning and getting to know the students, as it may be possible that three students in any one lesson need considerably more attention, care and understanding just to cope with the day-to-day situation of the classroom.

So far, I have discussed the typical pressures that students are facing, the effect that life in general and the way they are growing up is having upon them, and the methods that they use to cope with the emotional impact of those issues. Students bring these pressures to school every day, and the effects are going to be exaggerated within the structure of your lessons – it is vital that you are physically and, more importantly, mentally prepared to deal with them.

Poor behaviour has a variety of causes and sometimes the way it is dealt with is just as poor, echoing methods used by our forebears, isolating or ostracising those who don't conform to the expected norm. Thankfully, we have come a long way since those days, yet I still meet teachers and those in authority in schools who prescribe a one-size-fits-all way of dealing with poor behaviour, viewing it as a deliberate act of disobedience from the student. There is an alarming presumption that a student's attitude can be 'corrected' by simply putting that student into isolation for a few days or issuing detentions. If this doesn't work then the punishment gets increasingly harsh, often in proportion to the adult's annoyance.

Critical questions

» Do you take into account the mental stability and outside influences that can impact students when you are confronted with poor behaviour?

» What is the disciplinary policy within the school and how is it used?

» Is it your first port of redress or do you use it along with establishing an informative relationship with the student?

» What work do you do to restore relationships if the discipline policy has to be followed?

For some, the time to reflect on bad decisions or outbursts of poor behaviour can be beneficial, but we need to bear in mind that some students need more specialist methods of correction, support and guidance to help them.

I recently heard of one student who is now having treatment for bipolar disorder, but had to endure going through two schools and managed moves before her condition was recognised and she received the correct help and assistance. She is thankfully now able to access the learning she missed, but it shouldn't have taken so long to recognise her disorder.

Support staff

The deployment of TAs

Whenever I visit schools I am always interested in the provision and the effective deployment of TAs, to see how well they are included within the training and measures for school improvement, as I have found on occasions they are sadly overlooked. Yet their input into the smooth running of a classroom can at times be invaluable. Also, the knowledge they possess about students can assist teachers with differentiation and speed up the process of building a relationship with those who have difficulties coping with change and feel stressed at some of the things they have to face within an ordinary lesson. TAs can also provide very useful insights into students when writing reports, as the conversations they have on occasions within your class can be a rich source of information.

It is crucial for the school to have an effective SENCo/Inclusion Manager who understands the needs and capabilities of the TAs so that they can be deployed most appropriately.

The knowledge that the TA often holds regarding SEND students, their parents, outside agency provision, and the best way to teach them, as well as techniques of differentiation, is invaluable. My wife was an IM and I have watched how she managed and developed her team, developing resources for them as well as providing the vital information for teachers who can find themselves struggling to understand the needs of individual students. The way that teachers work with TAs is therefore a skill along with an understanding of SEND issues.

The role of the TA

You will be told by your school's SENCo which students in your class need specialist attention. The SENCo should also provide you with information relating to their specific needs. If you are fortunate enough to have a TA assigned to those students or generally available within your lessons, they are going to be a great asset to you and it is important that you learn to work with them effectively and, over time, look to building a good working relationship with them and their team.

If you have read the thoughts of the recent government *Reform* think tank, you will know that the role of the TA is under threat, because of the findings of Thomas Cawston, the think tank's research director, who said:

> We cited a swathe of evidence that questioned the value for money of teaching assistants and demonstrated that their impact on educational outcomes for pupils was negligible.

> We found that while they were supposed to help teachers, they were actually being allowed to take classes themselves. Not being prepared or qualified to do those classes, they were not doing a very good job.

> The money spent on teaching assistants would be far better spent on improving the quality of teachers.

Yet this only tells half the story, as the truth of the matter isn't that they are ineffective but that they are not *used* effectively.

Using your TA effectively

TAs are allocated by the SENCo or IM to support particular students, usually those with a EHCP, or specific SEND. However, the TA may also support other students who are underachieving once these individual students are on task. The TA should move around the room to support others, as this encourages independent learning, returning frequently to the SEND student to check progress

I recently asked a teacher who the person was who came into the lesson after five minutes and sat at the back. He said, *'To be honest I have no idea but she always comes in for this lesson.'*

Thankfully, this is a very rare occurrence and teachers do know the TA who frequents their lesson and will be able to name the SEN students the TA supports.

Communication is key when working with your TA. Find out when they can meet with you to discuss students and your scheme of work so they can know in advance what it is you want them to be working on. If you allow the TA to work with your higher-achieving students, you will have the opportunity to work with the SEN students. You only see the students in your lesson, whereas the TA may follow them through several lessons and will know the best ways to get them to work to their potential.

When giving your objective at the beginning of your lesson, have the TA stand at the front with you, showing the class the resources they will need, writing key words on the board or showing the 'stuck' strategies. This empowers the TA in the eyes of the class as equal to you, the teacher, in being able to support them.

TAs have frequent training in how to make the student an independent learner, so they should not be stuck by the SEN student's side for the whole lesson, but be able to move around, supporting other groups and checking in with the assigned students every five or ten minutes or so. Also, many TAs run interventions within their department for SEN students and very low achievers, usually extra Literacy or Numeracy coaching. It would be beneficial for you to know what interventions students from your lesson have as it is often possible to bridge across this learning.

TAs are the most expensive resource within a school, so if you are lucky enough to have one, try to build up a good relationship and use their skills to further support your students. If they do not have prep times, you can often arrange between you some time they can use to build up resources to help those who often get 'stuck'.

Partnership within the classroom

Establish first who the TA is working with, what specialist knowledge they have about both the subject you are teaching and the student they are working with. You may well be pleasantly surprised at the level of knowledge and expertise this person is bringing into your lesson. Quite a number of people apply to become a TA as a stepping stone towards a teaching career and working with them as they develop their skills can be very rewarding.

Let them know beforehand what you are aiming to teach over the coming term and find out the preferred learning method of the students for whom they are responsible.

Find out as much as you can about the student and, if possible, have the TA introduce the student to you before the lesson. This may require a special time but will only take a few moments and will help enormously in settling the student and dealing with their anxieties about meeting new people. Also take the time to find out what experience the student has in the topic that you are teaching and what they are concerned about for the coming term. Some students are very good at letting you know what they are bad at and can't do, and it is good to talk about successes they may have had in the past and the way that you will be looking after them in the future.

The TA will know what works and what levels the student can work at and it's important that you listen and respond to their advice, as this will save you a lot of work in the long run.

Talk with the TA and the student about social and emotional targets that you can all be working on as well as the academic ones. For example, it might be good to see if they can develop their group-work skills, or listening skills, or if they can become more independent and self-controlled. All of these targets need to be considered and, if appropriate, will go a long way to using school time effectively for them to develop greater independence. The TA will have a good idea of what the student struggles with socially as well as academically, and if it is possible for you to use your time with them to help, then it is a shame not to.

At times, the TA in the classroom can become almost stuck sitting with an assigned student and it becomes impossible for them to be able to move around the class. The dependency that some students develop on their TA can over time become detrimental for their personal development and also can become just a habit rather than a benefit. What would be ideal is that, over time and with good coaching, the TA can help the other students with simple things and you can spend a little bit more quality time with those who have more specialist needs.

Students might get annoyed by the presence of the TA, even if they are required to meet their needs. Some students don't want to be seen as having to rely upon someone else and try to distance themselves from the support. This needs to be handled very sensitively and the student's attitude needs to be taken into account but measured against what is also needed for them to attain their best.

Sometimes other students who are confident and able within a group setting can offer additional support for them and keep the learning flowing, but you will need to monitor the effectiveness of this approach on both the student who is helping as well as the student who is receiving the assistance. The TA can then be freed to offer support elsewhere while you monitor the SEN student.

TA toolkit

My wife, Sonia Allen, introduced a toolkit for all her TAs. It contains not only generic pieces of equipment but specialist SEN resources that they can use at various stages of the lesson to help with the student having difficulties either concentrating or getting started. This means that these resources are to hand within your class to assist in accessing learning. This is what they have found useful and I am sure you will as well:

- coloured acetate overlays / reading rulers for those with dyslexic tendencies;

- tangles and rubber 'squeezies' for those with ADHD, who need something unobtrusive to fiddle with to help them focus;

- sentence starters and grammar reminders on laminated cards;

- different coloured whiteboard markers for those who struggle with black on white;

- tissues for tears (and dealing with too much lipstick!);

- different coloured sticky notes for writing key words and sticking on the desk (these can also be used as behaviour reminders – eg 'Focus!' 'Quiet please' – instead of frequent verbal instructions);

- a slim notebook, for words misspelled or not understood (the TA then tests them on these words next lesson, and this can also be used as a starter);

- bendy wipe board, markers and rubbers;

- effective questions, cut into groupings for ease of use: Analysis, Knowledge, Comprehension, etc. A proactive TA prints these out and laminates them onto card and uses them as 'stuck' strategies too;

- small timers to leave on the desk, eg:

  - 1 minute – to get your thoughts together and make a start

  - 2 minutes – time out to reflect on your behaviour and come back on task

  - 3 minutes – to finish off that paragraph, then I'll be back to help;

- faculty starters, for if the teacher is late or dealing with something.

The list of possible toolkit resources is endless and can be personal to the students the TA supports. A recent Ofsted inspector observing this in use at my wife's school said what a very useful resource it was.

Chapter reflections

» *Mental health issues are going to play a part within your lessons and the success or failure of your lessons will depend a great deal upon what you know about your students, their mental health issues, any Statements attributed to them, their reading ages and any other things that could be impacting upon their capacity to learn and be fully engaged.*

» *The TA will be key to helping you, as will the material you produce and the resources you have to hand to help at different times. Being prepared means in all things, not just in a basic lesson plan, and keeping in touch with the information that can be found around school will go a long way to helping you prepare appropriately.*

» *I find that complaints about the cost of TAs and suggestions that they should be dispensed with have far more to do with the fact that they are not used effectively. Used effectively, as suggested here, they are a valuable resource for any school to invest in for the assistance of both students and teachers.*

Next steps

I hope that the above material has proved helpful and has also helped in giving a greater understanding as to the needs and demands that are being placed upon teachers because of the approach to education that is meant to include all. For some, the anxiety and stress that this approach causes means that disruption within the class is inevitable and that also means that teachers will inevitably feel that they have somehow failed. But I want you to remember that things are never as simple as that. You have to look at what you are doing and what is possible and bear in mind that you are always doing your best for the students who are in front of you. With that attitude you will never be classed as a failure.

Over time, your skills will be developing and growing, as will inevitably your career. In the next, and final, chapter we will look at how we can transfer the skills learnt within the classroom to leadership opportunities outside of the classroom.

Taking it further

Training and Development Agency for Schools (2007) *Role and Context for Teaching Assistant Trainers.* [online] Available at: http://webarchive.nationalarchives.gov.uk/20130401151715/http://www.education.gov.uk/publications/eOrderingDownload/sec_role_context07.pdf.

This publication offers a useful insight into the role of teaching assistants.

References

Broyd, N (2013) *Rise in ADHD Drug Prescriptions.* [online] Available at: www.webmd.boots.com/add-adhd/news/20130813/rise-in-adhd-drug-prescriptions (last accessed 1 April 2014).

Collishaw, S et al (2004) Time Trends in Adolescent Mental Health. *Journal of Child Psychology and Psychiatry*, 45(8): 1350–62.

Green, H, McGinnity, A, Meltzer, H, et al (2005) *Mental Health of Children and Young People in Great Britain 2004.* London: Palgrave.

Kim-Cohen, J, Caspi, A, Moffitt, T E, et al (2003) Prior Juvenile Diagnoses in Adults with Mental Disorder. *Archives of General Psychiatry*, 60: 709–17.

Mental Health Foundation (2006) *Truth Hurts: Report of the National Inquiry into Self-Harm Among Young People.* London: Mental Health Foundation

National Autistic Society (2014a) *What is Autism?* [online] Available at: www.autism.org.uk/about/what-is/asd.aspx (last accessed 13 June 2018).

National Autistic Society (2014b) *What Is Asperger Syndrome?* [online] Available at: www.autism.org.uk/about/what-is/asperger.aspx (last accessed 13 June 2018).

NHS (2013) *Autism Spectrum Disorder (ASD).* [online] Available at: www.nhs.uk/conditions/autism (last accessed 3 July 2018).

Nuffield Foundation (2013) *Social Trends and Mental Health: Introducing the Main Findings.* London: Nuffield Foundation.

Office for National Statistics (1997): *Psychiatric Morbidity Among Young Offenders in England and Wales.* London: Office for National Statistics.

Sempik, J et al (2008) Emotional and Behavioural Difficulties of Children and Young People at Entry into Care. *Clinical Child Psychology and Psychiatry*, 13(2): 221–33.

YoungMinds (2011) *100,000 Children and Young People Could Be Hospitalised Due to Self-Harm by 2020 Warns YoungMinds.* London: YoungMinds.

YoungMinds (2014) *Mental Health Statistics.* [online] Available at: https://youngminds.org.uk/about-us/media-centre/mental-health-stats (last accessed 12 June 2018).

9 Developing your own leadership style

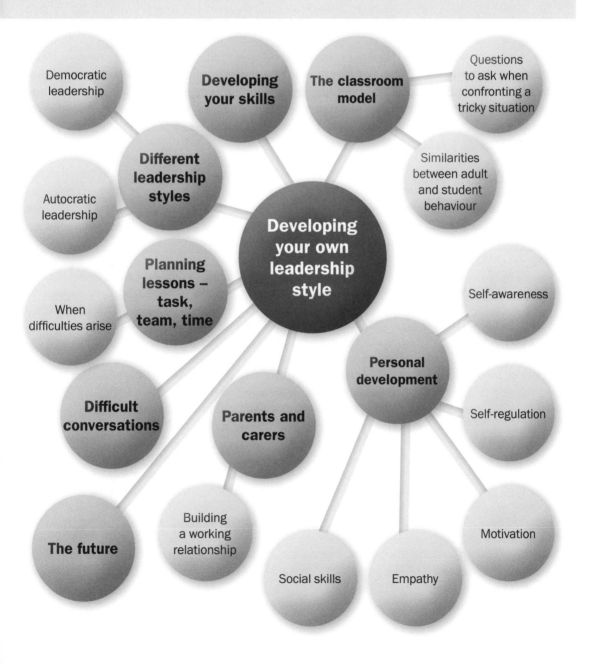

- Democratic leadership
- Developing your skills
- The classroom model
- Questions to ask when confronting a tricky situation
- Different leadership styles
- Autocratic leadership
- Similarities between adult and student behaviour
- Planning lessons – task, team, time
- Developing your own leadership style
- Self-awareness
- When difficulties arise
- Personal development
- Difficult conversations
- Parents and carers
- Self-regulation
- The future
- Building a working relationship
- Motivation
- Social skills
- Empathy

Introduction

> *The art of a good leader is getting people to do what they don't want to do and enjoy doing it.*
>
> Abraham Lincoln

I often use this quotation when delivering talks to teachers as I think it epitomises what teachers everywhere are having to do, sometimes on a daily basis. It highlights that, as teachers, you need to be leaders, but it is how you develop and use your leadership status that will be the measure of how successful you are going to be as a teacher.

Throughout this book, I have given you some guidance that can and should be used by all people who are in positions of leadership. But remember that leadership doesn't automatically come with a job title – it is what others bestow upon you. I have been into many a classroom where sadly I have seen the students taking the leadership role because the teacher hasn't been able to do so. No amount of shouting, threatening, pleading or encouraging will change the situation and enable you to lead if you haven't got the confidence or respect of the people you are seeking to lead. That is a shame but a reality for both the teacher and the students.

Developing your skills

Teaching, therefore, is going to be about you developing your skills as a leader. Those skills you develop within the classroom can be transferred to other aspects of leadership roles as you seek to work your way up within the educational sector.

CASE STUDY

I recently assisted a deputy head who had been given the task of overseeing a failing science faculty. I asked him what his plans were and he said he was going to first look at what his teachers didn't do well and get help for them, and then see what he could do by taking away some of their work load. His involvement and work load was going to be heavy as he was envisaging bearing the teachers' burdens to start with.

I asked him to imagine that the science faculty was his new class. How much work would he do for the students? What would be his first task with the new students? He said he would talk about a vision for the whole class, where he was going to get them; he would spend time getting to know the students, finding out who was good at things and who was struggling, and then tell them that he was going to be there with them along the learning journey, helping, inspiring, encouraging and empowering the students to do their best. I asked him how quickly he would do those things and he said straight away.

I also asked him to think about the science faculty and why he saw it as any different from a class that had lost its way, with some doing better than others and some who had lost interest or were demotivated. Like with the new class, he has to find out what the blocks are for the teachers so they can, with his help, overcome their barriers and do their best.

The teacher's role is to impart knowledge by helping others to understand things, and use that information to overcome issues and explore possibilities in the future with their new-found ability and belief. In effect, you become their coach as well as their teacher while they are with you. The role of a leader is to get the very best out of the team to inspire and encourage, leading by example, so that they achieve their full potential within their vision.

The role of a leader and a teacher is not to do things that the others find difficult but to find out the reasons why they find them difficult and then help them overcome them.

The classroom model

In previous chapters I have tried to help you understand your students and the issues they face and your responsibility towards them, helping you find ways to enable students to do their best. These skills are the same when you have to tackle any personnel issue in the future. You start with understanding how the situation has got to where it is, be that a department, a faculty, a classroom, or a school – even a business or personal issue – and from that point, seek to know those involved to help move things towards a better conclusion.

The strong BASE of belonging, autonomy and maintaining self esteem that you can create in your working relationships with colleagues as well as in the classroom will be the foundation on which you should build.

Questions to ask when confronting a tricky situation

If you have a very tricky situation to deal with then you have to look at the past influences that have impacted and shaped the people involved.

Then you need to use your emotional intelligence to take into account all the things that are affecting the people now. Here are the types of questions you can ask yourself.

- What are the interactions and relationships like?
- Who are the main players?
- Do they have any specific needs?
- What personality types are they?
- What part are you going to play to help move them on emotionally?
- What skills do you need to develop to help with moving things on?
- What vision will you present to them as they work with or for you?
- How are you going to challenge poor behaviour?
- What other things or people do you have to consider?
- Do all I work with feel a sense of belonging with me and each other?
- Have I looked at times when I can build autonomy into the learning?
- Have I looked at times when I can build autonomy into classroom management?

Think about some of the issues that you face within a classroom and see how they correspond to the people you meet as adults.

Similarities between adult and student behaviour

I often think that some of the issues I encounter with adults, for example their rudeness, emotional bullying, arrogant attitude, should have been dealt with at an early age. There are far too many adults who have missed out on their time on the naughty step.

With all the situations below substitute the word student with colleague.

- a student who can't be asked to do the work as they don't see the point;

- a student who always uses sarcasm to intimidate or belittle others;

- a student who doesn't want to follow the rules and procedures;

- a student who arrives late;

- a student who seems to be falling behind with their work;

- a student who doesn't get on with others;

- a student who doesn't work to their potential.

The list could go on, and all the time as a teacher you will be experimenting and finding things that work to encourage and guide. Using the tips from this book, along with finding and developing your skills over time, you will be training yourself to take on leadership roles.

Personal development

So what things do you need to develop and be aware of as an emotionally intelligent leader?

Daniel Goleman (2005) highlighted five attributes of emotional intelligence and it's a valuable exercise to examine these in more detail for yourself in a leadership role.

Self-awareness

Examine your own strengths and weaknesses, be aware of your tone, your motivation, your stress levels, and watch how and when your body is telling you things are getting out of hand. Some people suffer from dry skin, others high blood pressure, aching muscles, disruptive sleep patterns. Your body has a way of letting you know you are stressed before you recognise it, so respond to the signals by taking time out or getting help and advice about how to change things. Being self-aware also means examining your motivations and the causes of your frustrations. Reflect upon how you sound, your tone, your confidence and when you find an area that needs improving or developing, look for advice and guidance to allow you to do so. Don't be afraid to admit when you get it wrong and apologise.

Self-regulation

Check you are not compromising your basic principles when dealing with others. Learn to stay calm and find a way of stepping back when things get too emotional. Get your work–life balance sorted so that you can escape from very draining situations. Sometimes the demands are such that you may have to compromise your quality time with family and friends, but recognise that doing so can only be for a short time, otherwise something else will have to give. Learn to say no, and learn also to listen to both your heart and your head. Learn that you can't solve everything but you can play a meaningful part sometimes. Monitor what you eat and drink, and make sure that you look after the way you fuel your body. Also take care to relax your body as you need to maintain it well for the work you expect it to do. These are simple but easily overlooked words of advice that cause you to be mindful about yourself, and which will enable you to be mindful of others.

Motivation

Self-motivation is a very necessary tool for a leader as you have to keep reminding yourself why you are doing the job and what goal you are aiming for. With the demands to meet targets and the need to be prepared for the Ofsted inspection, it is too often the case that teachers lose sight of what is most important. I once asked a student to tell me the most important things that the school stood for and wanted from its students. He replied it was having your top button done up and your tie straight, as that was what they *'all keep going on about'*.

If you find yourself struggling, ask yourself why. And keep asking yourself that question until you unearth the real reason.

*   I am unhappy with my work. Why?
*   Because they don't do as I ask. Why?
*   Because they do their own thing when I speak. Why?
*   Because they aren't interested in what I say. Why?
*   Because they don't see the point of the work I am asking them to do. Why?

Eventually you get to a point where you have unpicked the whys and can see your direction more clearly. Keep your enthusiasm when those around you may be struggling. I often remind people of the saying *If you can't change the situation then change your attitude*. Look for the good in others and the situation. With everything that goes wrong you can either beat yourself or teach yourself. Be the example that others should follow. Keep that smile, it is infectious. Be a person you would want to meet.

Empathy

If you want to lead others then show them you genuinely care; don't just show it but truly mean it. Remember, you are only as strong as the weakest link within your team, and as a leader, you need to develop the skills of empathising with and understanding others, watching for and spotting the weakest link. People will show you they are the weakest link through their tone of voice or body language. Read those signs and keep on demonstrating your genuine interest and care. Always remember that people are different. It seems an obvious statement, but so often I hear people saying, *'Well, if they only did this'* or *'I was surprised they did that'*, as if they believe that others should always see things from their point of view. Other people will not always think the same as you, see things in the same way, or agree with you, but ultimately they need to know that your integrity and care for them is based upon your empathy with them. Don't just guess or assume that things are going well. Ask them. There is still a lot of truth in the adage *Assume makes an ASS out of U and ME*. Misunderstandings often lead to poor relationships and are usually caused by interpreting others' actions in the light of what you would have done in a similar experience.

Another lovely quotation from Abraham Lincoln is *'I don't like that man, I must try to get to know him better.'*

Social skills

In any walk of life, and especially in working with others, your social skills are going to determine your success or failure.

CASE STUDY

I worked with a mathematics teacher who didn't see the importance of building relationships with his students, and definitely didn't think there was a need to offer them a vision of what they were working towards. He said the best teacher he had was one who just told him if he was right or wrong, and who helped him by telling him what to do if he got it wrong. He tried to deliver his lessons following the same principle, and if the students didn't listen to him then he eventually sent them out. They were there to learn from him. He had the knowledge, and the method, all they had to do was listen and do it. I am sure I don't need to tell you that his lessons often degenerated into arguments and a power struggle as no attempt at relationships was being made.

Develop your communication skills as well as your listening skills. You have a message to give and your audience will give you clues as to why they do not understand. The only sure method of knowing someone has heard your message is to get them to repeat their understanding of what you have said.

Get to know the movers and shakers within your classroom as well as the school. Both will help you develop the feel of the class and the school and enable you to do your work more effectively and efficiently.

Develop your praising methods; decide what you are going to praise and when you are going to praise. Remember those who sometimes get overlooked yet play a great part in the smooth running of the school, for example those in the admin office, in reprographics, who clean and maintain the school. Don't take for granted their work just as you don't take for granted those who come into your class and do the simple correct things. We don't praise often enough, in my opinion. And, by the way, well done for getting this far with the book. I know of one head teacher who personally writes a penned letter to every individual member of staff over the year, thanking them for their contribution to the school, and posts it to their address.

Critical questions

Self-awareness

»   *Are you able to read your emotions and recognise when you need to rein in on things as well as when to let your emotions be shown?*

»   *Can you be honest with yourself about your own strengths and weaknesses and know how to manage both?*

»   *Do you inspire confidence born of your own self-confidence?*

Self-regulation

»   *Can you temper your emotions to a given situation?*

»   *Are you clear as to your motives and intentions with others so as to maintain your integrity?*

»   *Can you manage change and not get unsettled?*

»   *Can you allow others time to adapt to change and not get impatient?*

»   *Can you maintain high standards and not get influenced by others?*

»   *Can you be bold when you need to be as well as silent when the need also arises?*

Motivation

»   *Can you self-motivate?*

»   *Do you ask others what their motivational factors are?*

»   *Do you look for the positives in all things?*

»   *Can you be motivated to have those tricky conversations?*

Empathy

»   *Do you empathise with others and actively find out about others' concerns?*

»   *Are you able to recognise the needs in others and find ways of meeting them?*

»   *Are you able to respond to body and voice tone?*

Social skills

»   *Are you good at developing and maintaining relationships?*

»   *Can you be visionary and inspiring to others?*

»   *Can you respond positively to criticism?*

»   *Do you understand the importance of knowing the movers and shakers within the school?*

»   *Are your communications clear and convincing when dealing with all types of people?*

These are a few of the questions that you can reflect upon as you seek to develop your leadership skills and style.

Different leadership styles

Whenever I have watched an outstanding classroom I have seen teachers who have total control of the class flit from one form of leadership to another, choosing almost instinctively when to change their style. Sometimes they are directing and being autocratic and at other times they are guiding, asking students specific well-informed questions as they move towards a specific answer. On other occasions, the teacher allows the students to lead – even though the answers are in fact moving in the wrong direction. The teacher will let the students realise when they have gone wrong, and then guide them, helping them to see where they went wrong and get back on the right track. The leadership style may on occasions even mean that the students are ahead of the teacher. I once watched a Year 13 higher mathematics class in which a student who had been working on projects online wanted to show the teacher what he had learnt, and the teacher wanted to be shown as he hadn't seen it done before.

Whatever style you are using, remember that ultimately you are always the one making the final decision and remaining in charge. Your ultimate success will depend upon you being flexible and using a variety of leadership skills, the ability to understand others and clear communication. You must also be able to meet the needs and expectations of your students, your colleagues and the school for which you are working.

Stop for a moment and think about what words come into your mind when you think of the word 'boss'.

When you have come up with a few words, ask those who you teach and also your colleagues to talk about the variety of interpretations that people give to the word. This gives you some idea as to what others are thinking or expecting from you. You need to be able to fulfil their positive expectations as well as reassure them that you will not be fulfilling the negative aspects of the word.

> *Become the kind of leader that people would follow voluntarily, even if you had no title or position.*
>
> Brian Tracy (www.quoteswise.com/brian-tracy-quotes-9.html)

The key to successful leadership today is influence, not authority.
Kenneth Blanchard (www.kenblanchard.com/img/pub/Blanchard_Next_
Generation_of_Workers.pdf)

The challenge of leadership is to be strong, but not rude; be kind, but not weak; be bold, but not bully; be thoughtful, but not lazy; be humble, but not timid; be proud, but not arrogant; have humour, but without folly.
Jim Rohn (www.goodreads.com/author/quotes/657773.Jim_Rohn)

In each of these quotations you can substitute the word leader with teacher, and you should be aiming to develop all of these characteristics during your career.

Autocratic leadership

People with an autocratic style of leadership often demonstrate the following behaviour:

- They rely on their supposed power and position to get things done.

- They like people to acknowledge their status and power. There is a difference between encouraging respect by asking to be called Sir or Miss and demanding to be called Sir or Miss.

- They rarely change their mind once they have made a decision. To them it's a sign of weakness, yet in fact on occasions it can be seen as a sign of confidence.

If a classroom is led like this then you may well have control but you won't always be able to get the best of the students, as they will tend to feel demotivated. In some classrooms, it is important for you to demonstrate your authority, but that doesn't mean that you have to compromise building relationships. Instead, just establish that the pecking order of authority rests with you. I also find that a teacher with an autocratic style may have no trouble with students, but the next teacher has to try to counteract the poor attitude and lower morale this leadership style has caused.

I often get asked by people who have been promoted to lead a group or who have moved to a new school in a leadership position whether they should wait a few weeks and get to know their colleagues and then say what they have found they don't like, or whether they should start straight away. I ask them what would happen in a classroom if they did that. The same applies to adults. To try and change things after a few weeks will only cause resentment and create a bigger problem. Deal with things straight away in a calm but authoritative manner, with a measured, confident tone and follow through with any statements of correction or explanation that have been made.

Critical questions

» *What is your motivating factor for being an autocratic leader?*

» *What is your response to an autocratic leader?*

» *Do you find this style of leadership difficult?*

» *Have you dealt with things straight away or hoped that things will improve?*

Democratic leadership

A democratic style of leadership is often used when the focus is on building a team by using the expertise of each member. Within the classroom, this can be used when looking to encourage the students to share their thoughts and ideas regarding a specific subject or topic. The aim is to involve people in the decision-making by proposing a plan and inviting comments but all the time maintaining your authority. This is, for some, a more comfortable approach when dealing with adults and works well as long as those with whom you are leading or working are doing what is expected of them to a standard that is acceptable to all. The problem often arises when not everybody is working to the same standard. This can be dealt with in the classroom by reminding the student what is expected of them and that you will look to see improvement in both their attitude and commitment. This is easier if you have established right from the outset the agreed vision that you are working towards, and this is often the set grades that a student is expected to make. With a work colleague this could again be set against the common aim and vision of the group or faculty or department. The method is always the same, to find out what the problem is, to see what the person's attitude is towards the problem and what skills they have to overcome it, and also to see if there is anything that you need to do to help them. Maintaining the relationship is important, but it is also your responsibility not to lose sight of the goal.

Planning lessons – task, team, time

When thinking about your lesson plans and working within a class as well as working with a group it is important to consider the task, the team and the time. These three key elements of leadership will fit neatly into the term or topic that you have to get through.

Think back to the three key ingredients mentioned in Chapter 4 (the 3 Ms: Model, Manageable and Meaningful) and make sure that the task is clearly defined and understood by all. Create clear lesson objectives which cover social as well as educational expectations. Set goals that fit in with the needs of the task.

Keep your students focused and engaged in the task at hand, constantly looking for areas to praise, confirm or use as examples of good practice. Be aware that at any time you may need to re-evaluate what is being done and judge whether you need to make any changes to your style. Maintain team spirit, encourage those who need it, challenge those who need it, but never let yourself be sidetracked from the task. These again are skills that you can transfer to all areas of life in which you will need to deal with teams.

Keep checking for understanding, look for those to whom you can delegate responsibilities and keep your own involvement in the task to the minimum.

Make sure that everyone contributes by giving a voice to the quiet ones as well as encouraging the talkative ones to listen more.

When difficulties arise

Difficulties tend to arise when you cannot, because of time constraints or lack of resources, fulfil your commitment to all. You will be able to narrow down the reasons why things have gone astray by looking at how these three elements were catered for. Was the task too hard, was the team not functioning as you wanted because of individual needs causing you to have to divert your attention, or was the time allowed too short? Any long-term deficiency will lead eventually to poor results.

So you will see that careful monitoring of those elements throughout your lesson, but, more importantly, when planning a lesson, will help you maintain your position of leadership as well as getting excellent results out of all you seek to lead. Transference of these skills is a simple process to managing adults. Therefore, recognise that every day is a school day for both you and the students as you learn about people and issues and the best way to deal with them.

You will find that the classroom is not only for the students and their future, it is going to be your classroom for your future as well.

Critical questions

» *How much do you take into account the three elements of leadership when planning a lesson?*

» *How could you implement them within your planning?*

» *Think back to a time you were involved in an unsuccessful session. Which of the three elements was either overlooked or too heavily emphasised?*

Difficult conversations

There will be times throughout your career when you have to be involved in difficult conversations with your students or with your adult colleagues. When this happens, it is important that you keep the conversation simple and to the point. Always keep in your mind the relationship you have with the other person, and the outcome for which you are aiming, and adjust your style to maintain and achieve these.

CASE STUDY

I once talked with a head teacher about the need for straight talking with a member of his staff, and he did very well by saying to the teacher 'I am giving you three choices: I can put you in Capability, which means you could be on a very short road to being asked to leave if you don't improve, or you could resign, or you could start doing your best.' *Short and to the point, bringing clarity to the situation. The teacher chose the third option and, with support and the realisation of the situation in mind, improved measurably and to the satisfaction of all.*

Time in the classroom often involves helping the students to recognise that their behaviour is leading them down a path which isn't going to be helpful for them in the long run.

Parents and carers

Throughout your career you will have a lot of contact with the parents or carers of the students you are teaching. This can be both rewarding and tricky on occasion, but remember that the sooner you develop a relationship that is built upon mutual respect and understanding, the better it will be. If possible, find time at the earliest opportunity to introduce yourself to them and outline your hopes and commitment to their child. Ask their opinion about how the school is doing in relation to their child and look for possible insights and information that will be helpful.

So often it is the case that the only contact with a parent or carer is to discuss their child's poor behaviour, which is never a good starting point for an introduction, and can build a negative relationship. Also, some parents' own experience of school may have been negative, and so only having contact about behavioural issues dredges up bad memories for them regarding their own school days.

Building a working relationship

Do your best to link with parents and carers and share the good things their children have done as often as possible. Become the encourager and supporter, as this will often reap its rewards when more difficult conversations need to be had. Find common ground and, especially during parents' evenings, talk about their child as a whole person, and not just in terms of academic achievement or levels of progress. As a parent, I was always far more interested in hearing that my daughters were polite, caring and supportive and had the right attitude before finding out what grades they were going to attain. I am sure that I am not the only parent who is more interested in the teacher knowing my children rather than them just being another statistic and member of a specific class.

Critical questions

»   *In what ways can you get to know parents and carers?*

»   *How often do you call or write home regarding good things and positive attitude shown by your students?*

»   *How much do you know about the personal vision or hopes of your students' parents and carers?*

The future

The educational field is forever changing, and the expectations for the students are constantly being reviewed. It is widely believed that today's primary school children will end up in jobs that haven't been invented yet. So what is your role going to be? Is it to teach students a subject or is it to help facilitate their learning to become valuable members of society? Is it to enable them to get at least three levels of progress in their chosen subjects or is it to help them understand themselves and others better? Is it only to give them the educational skills to move on to college, university or employment, or is it to ensure that once there they can engage and work with their colleagues well? Finally, is your role to help students unwrap their mind and explore the possibilities to learn, explore and contribute to the world, or is it to give them the resources to cope with all that the world hands to them and come out on top? I am sure you know that it is all of these things and more.

You have chosen the best career in the world to pass on knowledge to others, to equip people to grow emotionally, academically and socially, to explore with them what they believe and what makes them who they are. Will they always appreciate you, listen to you, thank you? No. But will they, if you do a good job, always remember you? Yes.

I can guarantee that there will be days when you will struggle and question your ability. I once asked, during a whole-school training day, for anyone to stand up if they have ever had a day when they believed that they weren't up to the job? Everyone in the hall stood up. I then asked them to look around and give each other a round of applause for being there and sticking at it.

We have looked at the importance of emotional intelligence for the development of our students, colleagues and ourselves. This generation and those to follow are being introduced at an alarming rate to issues that adults find hard to grasp and make sense of. We know that this is having a detrimental effect upon their emotional development, yet we also are aware that there are many great and wonderful opportunities out there for them if only they can access them.

They will only be able to access these opportunities if they have been equipped with the basic skills for life, how to handle their anger, how to resolve conflict, how to empathise and communicate effectively with others. One other thing I can assure you is, when emotional intelligence is taught through a natural course of events such as those that occur within your classroom, then academic achievement will also increase. As I have said, there is no greater task, no more pressing need than to have competent, committed, emotionally intelligent teachers assisting in the development of our young people. I trust that after reading this book you feel more equipped, more prepared and more determined to be a positive influence in young peoples lives. I wish you well in your endeavour to ground yourself in the best profession in the world. I am always interested in feedback and comments so please feel free to contact me at info@victorallen.co.uk or follow me on @victormirrordt.

May your patience always be with you.

Victor

Critical questions

» *What will you do differently after reading this book?*

» *What things will you seek to develop over the next year?*

» *What emotional targets are you going to set your classes over the next academic year?*

Chapter reflections

» The teaching profession offers many opportunities for advancement, not only in this country but – as the qualifications are thought of so highly around the world – in other countries too.

» All the qualities that you will be required to bring to any position of leadership are, I believe, found in the classroom. The skills you will be honing as a teacher will stand you in good stead.

» Remember that you will always be dealing with people and they will be always be bringing their emotions with them to work and to the classroom. You will need to manage your own emotions if you wish to deal with those of other people.

» How you talk to people and introduce tasks may influence how effectively they carry out those tasks. Choose wisely: are you going to be autocratic or democratic?

» Difficult conversations are only difficult if you doubt your integrity and vision. Keep things clear and open, allow people to respond to what you have to say.

Taking it further

Goffee, R and Jones, G (2006) *Why Should Anyone Be Led by You? What It Takes To Be An Authentic Leader*. Boston, MA: Harvard Business School Press.

Goleman, D (1999) *Working with Emotional Intelligence*. London: Bloomsbury.

Reference

Goleman, D (2005) *Emotional Intelligence: Why It Can Matter More than IQ*. New York: Bantam Books.

Index